The Art of Listening

· ERICH FROMM ·

The Art
of Listening

Foreword by
RAINER FUNK

CONTINUUM • NEW YORK

1994

The Continuum Publishing Company
370 Lexington Avenue
New York, NY 10017

Printed in the United States of America

Library of Congress Cataloging-in-Publication Data

Fromm, Erich, 1900–1980
    The art of listening / Erich Fromm : edited by Rainer Funk.
        p.   cm.
    Includes bibliographical references and index.
    ISBN 0-8264-0654-8
    1. Psychoanalysis. 2. Listening—Psychological aspects.
I. Funk, Rainer. II. Title.
BF109.F76A5 1994
150.19'57—dc20   94-9102
                                                          CIP

Contents

Editor's Foreword

Erich Fromm became known to many people as a therapist. For more than 50 years, he practiced psychoanalysis; for more than 40 years, he was active in New York and Mexico City as a teacher, supervisor, and university lecturer at institutes for psychoanalytic teaching and training. Anyone who was in psychoanalysis with him sensed his relentlessness as a seeker of truth and as a critical companion as well as his extraordinary capacity for empathy, his closeness, and the immediacy of his relationship to others.

Although Fromm time and again had plans to write and publish about his particular therapeutic method, those plans were never realized. Thus, reports about Fromm's manner of interacting with patients who sat across from him and with analysts or colleagues in training are of lasting value. One should mention, above all, the works of R. U. Akeret (1975), G. Chrzanowski (1977, 1993), R. M. Crowley (1981), D. Elkin (1981), L. Epstein (1975), A. H. Feiner (1975), A. Gourevitch (1981), A. Grey (1992, 1993), M. Horney Eckardt (1975, 1982, 1983, 1992), J. S. Kwawer (1975, 1991), B. Landis (1975, 1981, 1981a), R. M. Lesser (1992), B. Luban-Plozza and U. Egles (1982), M. Norell (1975, 1981), D. E. Schecter (1971, 1981, 1981a, 1981b), J. Silva Garcia (1984, 1990), R. Spiegel (1981, 1983), E. S. Tauber (1959, 1979, 1980, 1981, 1981a, 1982, 1988), E. S. Tauber and B. Landis (1971), E. G. Witenberg (1981), B. Wolstein (1981), as well as contributions by Fromm's Mexican students that appeared in the journal *Revista de Psicoanálisis, Psiquiatría y Psicología* from 1965 to 1975 and in subsequent publications (*Memoria, Anuario*) of the Psychoanalytic Institute in Mexico, which Fromm founded. The contributions by M. Bacciagaluppi (1989, 1991, 1991a, 1993, 1993a), M. Bacciagaluppi and R. Biancoli (1993), R. Biancoli (1987, 1992), D. Burston (1991), M. Cortina (1992), R. Funk (1993), and L. von Werder (1990) draw on the works mentioned above and, in part, upon previously unpublished manuscripts by Fromm.

One can quickly list what Fromm himself published on questions pertaining to psychoanalytic therapy: a chapter concerning his understanding of dreams (in E. Fromm, 1951a), a piece concerning Freud's "The Case of Little Hans" (E. Fromm, 1966k), and reflections concerning therapeutic-technical questions (scattered throughout E. Fromm, 1979a, as well as in the section "The Revision of Psychoanalytic Therapy" in E. Fromm, 1990a, pp. 70-80). Richard I. Evans' 1963 interview with Fromm concerning questions about Fromm's concept of therapy, which appeared in English, Italian, and several other languages and which Evans published against Fromm's will (E. Fromm, 1966f), cannot serve as a source, since it "in my [Fromm's] judgment does not give any useful insight into my work" and represents "neither an introduction nor an 'overview' into the work." Some statements concerning therapeutic method that Fromm made in this interview were transcribed from tape word for word and included in the present volume.

The posthumously published texts in this volume are not a textbook about psychoanalytic therapy; nor are they a substitute for Fromm's nonexistent exposition of so-called psychoanalytic technique. It is no coincidence that Fromm did not write a textbook about psychoanalytic therapy and did not establish his own school of therapy. The special aspect of his therapeutic method cannot be encompassed in a "psychoanalytic technique" and the psychoanalyst cannot hide behind the "know how" of providing therapy.

The present volume does not inform about psychoanalytic technique; indeed, in Fromm's opinion, and against the claim of textbooks about psychoanalytic technique, there can be no such thing. However, the texts in this volume provide information about Fromm the therapist and his way of dealing with the psychological sufferings of people of our time. His therapeutic method is characterized not by verbose theories and abstractions, nor by differential diagnostic "rapes" of the "patient material," but rather by his capacity for individual and independent perception of the basic problems of man. Fromm's humanistic view permeates his ideas about patients and how to deal with them. The patient is not seen as being opposite; the patient is not a fundamentally different person. A profound solidarity is discernible between the analyzer and the analyzed. It assumes that the analyst has learned how to deal with him- or herself and is still ready to learn rather than to hide behind a "psychoanalytic technique." The analyst is his own next patient, and, for him, his patient becomes his analyst. Fromm can take the patient seriously because he takes himself seriously. He can analyze the patient because he analyzes himself by the counter-transference reactions the patient arouses in him.

None of the texts published in this volume existed in manuscript form, but rather only as English-language transcripts of recordings of lectures, interviews, and seminars. I have attempted to preserve the character of the spoken word of texts that, published here for the first time, were usually delivered without lecture notes. With the exception of the last section, the division and the sequence of the texts and headings were chosen, i.e., added, by me. Otherwise, I have indicated important additions in the text by brackets. The English transcripts are available in the Erich Fromm Archives (Ursrainer Ring 24, D-72076, Tübingen, Germany).

The first part of the present volume bears the title "Factors Leading to Patient's Change in Analytic Treatment" and constitutes the text of a lecture that Fromm held on September 25,

1964, on "The Causes for the Patient's Change in Analytic Treatment" at the Harry Stack Sullivan Society on the occasion of the dedication of the new building of the William Alanson White Institute in New York. This lecture is particularly outstanding because Fromm distinguishes between benevolent and malevolent neurosis and very clearly shows the limits of psychoanalytic treatment. (See also E. Fromm, 1991c, in which this was previously published in part.)

The second part ("Therapeutic Aspects of Psychoanalysis") contains excerpts from a seminar that Fromm, together with Bernard Landis, gave for American psychology students during a three-week seminar in Locarno in 1974. In subsequent years, the transcript of this seminar, which weighed in at 400 pages, was prepared by his secretary, Joan Hughes, on the basis of recordings and was then partially revised by Fromm. Fromm originally intended to incorporate parts of this transcript in a book about psychoanalytic therapy. The first part of this book was supposed to deal with the limitations of Freudian understanding. Fromm wrote the manuscript for this after he finished *To Have or To Be?* in 1976 and 1977. The second part, for which he revised the transcript of the 1974 seminar, was supposed to deal with questions about therapeutic method. However, a severe heart attack in the autumn of 1977 thwarted his continued work on this, such that the first part, the discussion of Freud's psychoanalysis, was finally published independently of the planned second part in 1979 (see E. Fromm, 1979a).

The portions of the transcript of the 1974 seminar published here provide firsthand information not only about the therapist Fromm (information that is enriched especially by his remarks about a case report brought up in the seminar by Bernard Landis), but also about his perception of modern character neuroses and of the necessity of special requirements in their treatment. Some sections of the 1974 seminar were expanded by statements that Fromm made in 1963 in the interview already mentioned. The final section, which bears the title formulated by Fromm himself, "Psychoanalytic 'Technique'—or the Art of Listening," was written by him shortly before his death in 1980 and was supposed to introduce the publication of portions of the 1974 seminar.

Tübingen, January 1994   Rainer Funk

(Translated by Lance W. Garmer)

· PART I ·

Factors Leading to Patient's Change in Analytic Treatment

· 1 ·

Curing Factors According to Sigmund Freud and My Critique

When speaking about factors leading to analytic cure, I think the most important work written on the subject was Freud's paper *Analysis, Terminable and Interminable* (1937c), which is one of his most brilliant papers, and, if one could put it that way, one of his most courageous papers, although Freud never lacked in courage in any of his other work. It was written not long before his death, and in a way it is Freud's own last summarizing word about the effect of analytic cure. I first shall summarize briefly the main ideas of this paper and then, in the main part of this lecture, try to comment on it and possibly make some suggestions in connection with it.

First of all, what is interesting in this paper is that Freud presents in it a theory of psychoanalysis which had not really changed since the early days. His concept of neurosis is that neurosis is a conflict between instinct and the ego: either the ego is not strong enough, or the instincts are too strong, but at any rate, the ego is a dam; it is not capable of resisting the onrush of instinctual forces, and for this reason neurosis occurs. This is in line and consequent with his early theory, and he presented it also in its essence without trying to embellish or modify it. What follows from that is that analytic cure consists essentially in strengthening the ego which in infancy was too weak, enabling it to cope now with instinctual forces, in a period in which the ego would be strong enough.

Secondly, what according to Freud is cure? He makes it very clear, and I may quote here from *Analysis, Terminable and Interminable* (1937c; S.E., vol. 23, p. 219): "First the patient"—provided we speak of cure—"shall no longer be suffering from his [former] symptoms and shall have overcome his anxieties and his inhibitions." There is another very important condition. Freud does not assume that cure of the symptoms, disappearance of the symptoms per se, constitutes cure. Only if the analyst is convinced that enough unconscious material has been brought to the surface, which would explain why the symptoms have disappeared [naturally in terms of the theory]—only then can the analyst be convinced that the patient is cured, and is not likely to have repetitions of his former symptoms. Actually, Freud speaks here of a "taming of the instincts" (cf. loc. cit., p. 220). The analytic process is a taming of the instincts or, as he also says, making the instincts more "accessible to all the influences of the other trends in the ego" (loc. cit., p. 225). First, the instincts are brought to awareness because how can you tame them otherwise?—and then in the analytic process the ego becomes stronger and gains the strength which it failed to acquire in childhood.

Thirdly, what are the factors which Freud mentioned in this paper as determining the results of analysis—either cure or failure? He mentions three factors: first, "the influence of traumas"; secondly, "the constitutional strength of the instincts"; and thirdly, "the alterations of the ego" in the process of defense against the onrush of the instincts (cf. loc. cit., p. 225).

An unfavorable prognosis, according to Freud, lies in the constitutional strength of the instincts, plus or combined with a modification, an unfavorable modification of the ego in the defense conflict. It is well known that for Freud the constitutional factor of the strength of instinct was a most important factor in his prognosis for a patient's cure in an illness. It is a strange thing that Freud throughout his work, from the early writings on until this very latest of his writings, emphasized the significance of constitutional factors, and that neither the Freudians nor the non-Freudians have done more than paying lip service at the very most to this idea, which for Freud was very important.

So, Freud says one unfavorable factor for cure is the constitutional strength of the instincts, even, he adds, if the ego is normally strong. Secondly, even the ego modification, he says, can be constitutional. In other words, he has a constitutional factor on two sides: on the side of the instincts and on the side of the ego. He has a further factor which is unfavorable, and that is that part of the resistance which is rooted in the death instinct. That, of course, is an addition which comes from his later theory. But naturally, in 1937, Freud would consider also that as one factor unfavorable to cure.

What is the favorable condition for cure according to Freud? This is something which many people are not aware of when they think of Freud's theory, namely, that according to this paper of Freud's, the stronger the trauma the better are the chances for cure. I shall go into the question why this is so and why I think this was so in Freud's own mind, although he does not talk too much about it.

The person of the psychoanalyst is the other factor which hopefully is favorable to the cure. Freud makes here, in this last paper, a very interesting remark on the analytic situation which is worthwhile mentioning: The analyst, he says, "must possess some kind of superiority so that in certain analytic situations he can act as a model for his patient, and in others as a teacher. And, finally, we must not forget that the analytic relationship is based on a love of truth—that is, on a recognition of reality—

and that it precludes any kind of sham and deceit" (S. Freud, 1937c; S.E., vol. 23, p. 248). I think that is a very important statement Freud made here very clearly.

One last word about Freud's concept here, which he does not put explicitly but which is implicit and which goes through his whole work if I understand it correctly. Freud always had a somewhat mechanistic view of the process of cure. Originally the view was, if one uncovers or discovers the repressed affects then the affect by becoming conscious gets out of the system, so to speak; this was called abreacting, and the model was a very mechanical one, like getting pus out of an inflamed spot and so on, and it was supposed to be quite natural, quite automatic, that this happened.

Freud and many other analysts saw that this wasn't true because, if it were true, then the people who act out most their irrationality would be the healthiest ones because they would get the stuff out of their system—and they don't. So, Freud and other analysts gave up the theory. But this was replaced by the less explicit idea that the patient has insight, or, if you use another word, becomes aware of his unconscious reality, then his symptoms simply disappear. One does not really have to make a special effort, except the one to come, to free associate, and to go through the anxieties which this necessarily involves. But it is not a question of the patient's particular effort, particular will—he will get well provided one succeeds in overcoming the resistances, and the repressed material comes to the fore. This is by no means as mechanistic as Freud's original abreacting theory was. But it is still somewhat mechanistic, as I see it. It contains the implication that the process is a smooth one, in the sense that, if one uncovers the material, then the patient will get well in this process.

Now I want to make some further comments on, some additions to, and some revisions of these views of Freud on the causes which effect cure. First of all, I want to say that, if one asks what is analytic cure, then I think that what unites, or what is common to all psychoanalysts, is Freud's basic concept that *psychoanalysis can be defined as a method which tries to uncover the unconscious reality of a person* and which assumes that in this process of uncovering the person has a chance to get well. As long as we have this aim in mind, then a good deal of fighting among various schools would be somewhat reduced in importance. If one really has that in mind, one knows how very difficult and treacherous it is to find the unconscious reality in the person, and then one does not get so excited about the different ways in which one tries to do that, but one asks which way, which method, which approach is more conducive to this aim, which is the aim of all that can be called psychoanalysis. I would say that any therapeutic method which does not have that aim may be therapeutically very valuable; however, it has nothing to do with psychoanalysis, and I would make a clear-cut division right at this point.

As to Freud's concept that analytic work is like reinforcing a dam against the onrush of the instincts, I don't want to argue against this point, because I think many things can be said in favor of it. Especially, I believe, if we deal with the question of psychosis as against neurosis, then we really deal with the brittleness of the ego and the strange thing that one person does and another person does not collapse under the impact of certain impulses. So I'm not denying the validity of the general concept that ego strength has something to do with the process. But nevertheless, with this qualification, it seems to me that the main problem of neurosis and cure is precisely not that of here come the irrational passions and there is the ego which protects the person from becoming sick.

There is another contradiction, and that is the battle between two kinds of passion, namely, the archaic, irrational regressive passions as against other passions within the personality. I shall be a little more explicit to make myself understood. I mean by the archaic passions: intense destructiveness, intense fixation to the mother, and extreme narcissism.

By *intense fixation* I mean the fixation which I would call a symbiotic fixation, or which in Freudian terms one would call the pre-genital fixation to the mother. I mean that deep fixation in which the aim is really to return to the mother's womb or even return to death. I should like to remind you that Freud himself in his later writings stated that he underestimated the significance of the pre-genital fixation. Because in his whole work he put so much emphasis on the genital fixation, he therefore underestimated the problem of the girl. While for the boy it is plausible that all this should start with the erotic genital fixation to the mother, with a girl it doesn't really make sense. Freud saw that there is a great deal of pre-genital—that is to say, not sexual in the narrower sense of the word—fixation to the mother, which exists both in boys and girls and which he had not paid sufficient attention to in his work in general. But this remark of Freud's also got lost somewhat in the analytic literature, and when analysts speak about the Oedipal phase and the Oedipal conflict and the whole business, they usually think in terms of the genital, not of the pre-genital fixation or attachment to the mother.

By *destructiveness* I mean not destructiveness which is essentially defensive, in the service of life, or even secondarily in the defense of life, like envy, but destructiveness in which the wish to destroy is its own aim. I have called that necrophilia.[1]

[Strong mother fixation, necrophilic destructiveness, and extreme narcissism are malignant passions]—malignant because they are related to, they are causative of severe illness. Against these malignant passions you have also the opposite passions in man: the passion for love, the passion for the interest in the world—all that which is called Eros, the interest

---

1. Cf. E. Fromm, *The Heart of Man: Its Genius for Good and Evil*, 1964a, which deals precisely with this problem of what are the sources of, and what is really severe pathology.

not only in people, but also the interest in nature, the interest in reality, the pleasure in thinking, all artistic interest.

It is fashionable today to talk about what the Freudians call ego functions—which I think is a poor retreat and the discovery of America after it has been discovered for a long time, because nobody ever doubted outside of Freudian orthodoxy that there are many functions of the mind which are not the result of instincts in the sexual sense. I think by this new emphasis on the ego, one has done some retreat from that which was the most valuable part in Freud's thinking, namely, the emphasis on the passions. While ego strength in a certain sense is a meaningful concept, the ego is essentially the executor of the passions; it's either the executor of malignant passions or of benign passions. But what matters in man, that determines his action, what makes his personality, is what kind of passions move him. To give an example: It all depends on the question whether a person has a passionate interest in death, destruction, and all that is not alive, which I called necrophilia, or a passionate interest in all that is alive, which I call biophilia. Both are passions, both are not logical products, both are not in the ego. They are part of the whole personality. These are not ego functions. These are two kinds of passion.

This is a revision I would suggests with regard to Freud's theory: that *the main problem is not the fight of ego versus passions, but the fight of one type of passion against another type of passion.*

Benign and Malignant Neuroses—with a Case History of a Benign Neurosis

Before I go on to the question: what is analytic cure or what are the factors leading to analytic cure, naturally one has to consider and to think about the question: what kinds of neurosis are there? There are many classifications of neurosis and many changes in the classification. Dr. Menninger has recently suggested that most of these classifications have no particular value, without really suggesting a new one which has one and which he recommends as an essential classifying concept. I would like to suggest the following classification— this is a very simple one in a way—and that is the difference between benign neurosis and malignant neurosis.

A person suffers of a benign or light neurosis, if he or she is not essentially seized by one of these malignant passions, but whose neurosis is due to severe traumata. Here I am entirely in agreement with what Freud said, namely, that the best chances for cure lie precisely in those neuroses where the patient suffers from the most severe trauma. The logic is that if a patient survives a severe trauma without becoming psychotic or showing forms of sickness which are exceedingly alarming, then indeed he or she shows that from a constitutional standpoint he or she has a lot of strength. In those cases of neurosis in which what I like to call the nucleus of the character structure is not severely damaged, that is to say, is not characterized by these severe regressions, these severe forms of malignant passions, I think there analysis has its best chances. Naturally, it requires work in which whatever the patient has repressed has to be clarified, has to come to consciousness; that is to say: the nature of the traumatic factors, the reactions of the patient to these traumatic factors—which have, as is very frequent, denied the real nature of the traumatic factor.

I want to illustrate a *benign neurosis* with a short case history of a Mexican woman whose therapy I supervised. She is unmarried, about twenty five years old, her symptom is homosexuality. Since the age of eighteen she has only had homosexual relationships with other girls. At the point where she comes to the analyst she has a homosexual relationship with a cabaret singer, goes every night to hear her friend, gets drunk, is depressed, tries to get out of this vicious circle, and yet submits to this friend, who treats her abominably. Nevertheless, she is so frightened to leave her, she is so intimidated by the threat of the other woman to leave her, that she stays on.

Now, that's rather a bad picture: a case of homosexuality, but very much characterized by this constant anxiety, light depression, aimlessness of life, and so on. What is the history of this girl? Her mother was a woman who has been the mistress of a rich man for a long time. All the time she was the mistress of the same man, and this was the offspring of the relationship, the little daughter. The man was quite faithful in a way, always supporting the woman and the little girl, but he was not a father in evidence, there was no presence of a father. The mother, however, was an utterly scheming mother who only used this little girl to get money out of the father. She sent the girl to the father to get money out of him, she blackmailed the father through the girl, she undermined the girl in every way she could. The mother's sister was the owner of a brothel. She tried to induce the little girl into prostitution, and actually the little girl did, twice—she wasn't so little then—appear naked in front of men to be paid for it. It probably took a lot of stamina not to do more. But she was terribly embarrassed because, you can imagine, the children of the block, what names they called her, being quite openly not only a girl without a father, but also the niece of the owner of the brothel.

So the girl developed until the age of fifteen into a frightened, withdrawn girl, with no confidence in life whatsoever. Then the father, in one of his whims, sent her to school, to college in the United States. One can imagine the sudden change of scenery for this little girl, coming to a rather elegant college in the United States, and there was a girl who kind of liked her and was affectionate to her, and they started a homosexual affair. Now there is nothing amazing in that. I think it's quite normal that a girl so frightened, with a past like that, would start a sexual affair with anyone, man, woman, or animal, who shows real affection; it's the first time that she gets out of a hell. Then she has other homosexual affairs and she goes back to Mexico, goes back into that same misery, always with uncertainty, always with a feeling of shame. Then she hits on this woman I have spoken about who kept her in a state of obedience—and that's when she comes to the analyst.

What happened in analysis was—I think in the course of two years—that she first left this homosexual friend, she then stayed alone for awhile, then she began to date men, then she fell in love with a man, and then she married him and she isn't even frigid. Obviously this was not a case of homosexuality in any genuine sense. I say "obviously"—some may disagree with me—but in my own opinion this is as much homosexuality as probably most people have as potential.

This was actually a girl who—and one can see that from her dreams—was simply frightened to death by life; she was like a girl who comes from a concentration camp, and her expectations, her fears, were all conditioned by this experience. And in a relatively short time, considering the time usually required for analysis, this patient develops into a perfectly normal girl, with normal reactions.

I give this example just to indicate what I mean by, and what I think Freud means by, the strong role of trauma in the genesis of neurosis as against the constitutional factors. Of course I am aware of the fact that when Freud talks of trauma he means by this something different from what I would mean: he would look for a trauma essentially of a sexual nature; he would look for the trauma happening in an earlier age. I believe that very often the trauma is a prolonged process in which one experience follows another and where, really, you eventually have a summation, and more than a summation, a piling up of experiences—sometimes in a way which I think is not too different from war neurosis, where there comes a breaking point when the patient gets sick.

Nevertheless, the trauma is something which happens in the environment, which is a life experience, a real-life experience. This holds true for this girl and of these kinds of patients with traumas, where the nucleus of character structure is not basically destroyed. Although the picture can be quite severe on the outside, they have a very good chance to get well and to overcome the reactive neurosis in a relatively short time because constitutionally they are sound.

In this connection I want to emphasize that in the case of a benign or reactive neurosis the traumatic experience has to be quite massive to be an explanation for the genesis of neurotic illness. Is the trauma seen in a weak father and a strong mother? Then this "trauma" does not explain why a person suffers of a neurosis because there are many who have a weak father and a strong mother and don't become neurotic. In other words, if I want to explain neurosis by a traumatic event then I have to assume that the traumatic events are of such an extraordinary nature that it is unthinkable that there are cases with the same traumatic background who are perfectly well. Therefore I think in those cases, when one hasn't more to show than a weak father and a strong mother, one has to think of the probability that there are constitutional factors which are at work; that is to say, factors which make this person prone to neurosis and in which the role of the weak father and the role of the strong mother could become traumatic only because the constitutional factor tended to neurosis. Under ideal conditions such a person might not have become ill.

I'm not willing to accept the assumption that one person becomes very sick and that all my explanation is one which holds true for so many others who didn't become very sick. You find a family of eight children and one is sick and the rest aren't. Usually the rationale is: "Yes, but he was the first one, the second one, the middle one, God knows what…"—that's why his experience was different from the experience of all others. That is very nice for those who like to comfort themselves that they have discovered the trauma, but to me it is very loose thinking.

Naturally, it can be that there is a traumatic experience which we don't know, that is to say, which hasn't come up in the analysis. And if the analyst will have the skill to find that truly and extraordinarily strong traumatic experience and can show how this was essential for the development of neurosis, I am very happy. But I cannot simply call that a traumatic experience which in many other cases turns out not to be a traumatic experience. There are quite a number of traumatic experiences which are really extraordinary. That's why I gave this example.

There is one other instance which I just want to mention, which is a very modern phenomenon, and a very hard question to answer. How sick, really, is modern organization man: alienated, narcissistic, without relatedness, without real interest for life, with interest only for gadgets, for whom a sports car is much more exciting than a woman. Now, how sick is he then?

In one sense one could say he's quite sick, and therefore certain symptoms would follow: he is frightened, he is insecure, he needs constant confirmation of his narcissism. At the same time, however, one might say a whole society is not sick in that sense: people function. I think for these people the problem arises how they succeed in adapting themselves to the general sickness, or to what you might call the "pathology of normalcy." The therapeutic problem is very difficult in these cases. This man indeed suffers from a "nuclear" conflict, that is to say, from a deep disturbance in the nucleus of his personality: he shows an extreme form of narcissism and a lack of love of life. And yet to cure him he would in the first place have to change his whole personality. Besides that he would have almost the whole society against him, because the whole society is in favor of his neurosis. Here you have the paradox of having in a way a sick person theoretically, but who is, however, not sick in another sense. It's very difficult to determine what analysis could do in this case, and I really find this a tough problem.

To speak of what I call the benign neurosis, there the task is relatively simple, because you deal with intact nuclear energy structure, character structure; you deal with traumatic events which explain the somewhat pathological deformation. In the atmosphere of analysis, both in the sense of bringing out the unconscious plus the help which the therapeutic relation to the analyst is, these people have a very good chance to get well.

What I mean by the idea of *malignant neurosis* I have already said. These are neuroses where the nucleus of the character structure is damaged, where you have people with either extreme necrophilic, narcissistic, or mother-fixated trends, and usually, in the extreme cases, all three go together and tend to converge. Here, the job of cure would be to change the energy charge within the nuclear structure. It would be necessary for cure that the narcissism, the necrophilia, all the incestuous fixations change. Even if they do not change completely, even if there is a small energy charge in what the Freudians call the *cathexis* of these various forms, this would indeed make a great difference to the person. If this person were to succeed in reducing his narcissism, or in developing more of his biophilia, or in developing an interest in life and so on, then this person has a certain chance to get well.

If we speak of analytic cure, in my opinion one should be very aware of the difference of the chances for cure in the malignant cases and in the benign cases. One might say that is really the difference between psychosis and neurosis, but it isn't, really, because many of what I call here malignant character neuroses are not psychotic. I am talking here about a phenomenon which you find in neurotic patients with or without symptoms, who are not psychotic, who are not even near psychotic, who probably would never become psychotic, and yet where the problem of cure is an entirely different one.

What is different is also the nature of the resistance. You will find in a benign neurosis—after all the resistance born out of hesitancy, some fear and so on—that, since the nucleus of the personality is really normal, the resistance is relatively easy to overcome. If you take, however, the resistance of what I call the malignant, the severe neuroses, then the resistances are deeply rooted, because this person would have to confess to himself and to a lot of human beings that he or she is really a completely narcissistic person, that he really cares for nobody. In other words, he has to fight against insight with a vigor which is much greater than that of the person who suffers from a benign neurosis.

What is the method of cure in severe neurosis? I do not believe that the problem is essentially the strengthening of the ego. I believe the problem of cure lies in the following: that the patient confronts the irrational archaic part of his personality with his own sane, adult, normal part and that this very confrontation creates conflict. This conflict activates forces which one has to assume if one has the theory that there exists in a person—more or less strongly and, I think, again that is a constitutional factor—a striving for health, a striving for a better balance between the person and the world. *For me the essence of analytic cure lies in the very conflict engendered by the meeting of the irrational and the rational part of the personality.*

One consequence for analytic technique is that the patient must travel on two tracks in the analysis: he must experience himself as the little child, let us say, of two or three that he is unconsciously, but he must at the same time also be an adult responsible person who faces this part in himself, because in this very confrontation he acquires the sense of shock and the sense of conflict and the sense of movement which is necessary for analytic cure.

From this standpoint the Freudian method would not do. I think we find here two extremes: the Freudian extreme is that the patient is artificially infantilized by the situation of the couch, the analyst sitting behind and so on, the whole ritualism of the situation. Freud expected, and René Spitz explained this in an article, that this is the real purpose of the analytic situation, to artificially infantilize the patient so that more of the unconscious material comes up. I think this method suffers from the fact that in this way the patient never confronts himself with this archaic or infantile material; he becomes his unconscious, he becomes a child. What happens is, in a way, a dream, but in a waking state. All this comes out, all this appears, but the patient isn't there.

But it is not true that the patient is a little child. The patient (let us assume for the moment he is not a severe psychotic) is, at the same time, a normal, grown-up being, with sense, with intelligence, with all sorts of reactions which fit a normal being. Therefore he can react to this infantile being in him. If this confrontation doesn't take place, as it usually doesn't in the Freudian method, then indeed this conflict doesn't appear, this conflict isn't set in motion. In my opinion one of the main conditions for analytic cure is lacking.

The other extreme from Freud is that method of psychotherapy which is sometimes also called analysis and in which the whole thing degenerates into a psychological conversation between the analyst and the grown-up patient, where the child doesn't appear at all, where the patient is addressed as if there were none of these archaic forces in him, and where one hopes by a kind of persuasion, by being nice to the patient and telling him: "Your mother was bad, your father was bad, but I'm going to help you, you'll find yourself secure," that this will cure him. A neurosis which is very light may be cured that way, but I think there are shorter methods than five years. I think a severe neurosis is never cured unless you have, as Freud said, unearthed or uncovered sufficient unconscious and relevant material.

What I am proposing here is simply that the analytic situations both of the patient and in a sense of the analyst, is a paradoxical one, that the patient is neither only the child and the irrational person with all sorts of crazy fantasies, nor is he only the grown-up person with whom one can converse intelligently about his symptoms. The patient must in the same hour and at the same time be able to experience himself as both, and therefore experience the very confrontation which sets something going.

The main point as far as cure is concerned is for me the real conflict which is engendered in the patient by this confrontation. And this cannot be done in theory and this is not done just by words. Even if one takes a simple thing, as when a patient says: "I was afraid of my mother," what does that mean? That is the kind of fear we are all accustomed to; we are afraid of the schoolteacher, of a policeman, we are afraid that somebody might hurt us—that is nothing so world-shaking. But maybe what the patient means when he says he was afraid of his mother can be described, let us say, in these terms: "I am put into a cage. There is a lion in that cage. And somebody puts me in and closes the door, and what do I feel?" In dreams, this is exactly what comes up, namely, the alligator or the lion or the tiger trying to attack the dreamer. But to use words, "I was afraid of my mother," that falls short of the necessity to cope with the patient's real fear.

· 3 ·

Constitutional and Other Factors for Cure

I come now to some other factors, some favorable, some unfavorable. First of all, the constitutional factors. I indicated already that I believe the constitutional factors are terribly important. In fact, if you had asked me 30 years ago about the constitutional factors and I had heard something I am saying I would have been very indignant; I would have called this a reactionary or Fascist kind of pessimism which doesn't permit changes and what not. But in quite a few years of analytic practice I have convinced myself—not on any theoretical basis, because I don't even know anything about the theory of heredity, but by my experience—that it just isn't true to assume that we can account for the degree of neurosis as simply proportional to the traumatic and environmental circumstances.

It's all very nice if you have homosexual patients and you find out that the patient has a very strong mother and a very weak father, and then you have the theory that explains homosexuality. But then you have ten other patients who have just the same weak father and strong mother, and they don't turn out to be homosexual. You have similar environmental factors which have very different effects. And therefore I really do believe that, unless you deal with extraordinarily traumatic factors in the sense I was talking about before, you cannot really understand the development of a neurosis if you do not think of constitutional factors, in the sense that, either alone, because they are so strong, or at least in cooperation with certain conditions, certain constitutional factors make environmental factors highly traumatic and others do not.

The difference, of course, between the Freudian view and my own is that Freud thinks, when he talks about constitutional factors, essentially about instinctual factors, in terms of libido theory. I believe that constitutional factors go much further. I cannot try here to explain this any further right now, I think constitutional factors cover not only factors, which are usually defined as temperament—be it in the sense of the Greek temperaments or in the sense of Sheldon, but also factors such as vitality, love of life, courage, and many other things which I don't even want to mention. In other words, I think a person, in the lottery of the chromosomes, is already conceived as a very definite being. The problem of a person's life, really, is what life does to that particular person who is already born in a certain way. Actually, I think it's a very good exercise for an analyst to consider what would this person be if life conditions had been favorable to that kind of being he was conceived as, and what are the particular distortions and damages which life and circumstances have done to that particular person.

Among the favorable constitutional factors belong the degree of vitality, especially the degree of love of life. I personally think that one can have a rather severe neurosis, with a good deal of narcissism, even with a good deal of incestuous fixation, but if one has love of life then one has an entirely different picture. To give two examples: One is Roosevelt and the other is Hitler. Both were rather narcissistic, Roosevelt certainly less than Hitler but sufficiently so. Both were rather mother-fixated, probably Hitler in a more malignant and profound way than Roosevelt. But the decisive difference was that Roosevelt was a man full of love of life, and Hitler was a man full of love of death, whose aim was destruction—an aim which wasn't even conscious, because for many years he believed that his aim was salvation. But his aim was really destruction, and everything that led to destruction attracted him.—Here you see two personalities where you might say the factor of narcissism and the factor of mother fixation, while different, were markedly present. But what was entirely different was the relative amount of biophilia and necrophilia. If I see a patient who might be quite sick, but I see lots of biophilia, I am quite optimistic. If I see in addition to everything else very little biophilia but a good deal of necrophilia, I am prognostically quite pessimistic.

There are other factors which make for success or failure which I just want to mention briefly. They are not constitutional factors, and I think they can be tested pretty much in the first five or ten sessions of the analysis.

(a) One is whether *a patient has really reached the bottom of his suffering.* I know of one psychotherapist who only takes patients who have gone through every method of therapy which it is possible to find in the United States, and if no other method has worked, he accepts the patient. That, of course, could be a very nice alibi for his own failure—but in this case it is really a test, namely, that the patient has gone to the bottom of his suffering. I think it's very important to find that out. Sullivan used to stress this point very much, although in slightly different terms: the patient has to prove why he needs treatment. And by that he didn't mean the patient has to give a theory of his illness, or anything like that. Obviously he didn't mean that. He meant, the patient must not come with the idea: "Well, I'm sick. You are a professional who promises to cure sick people, here I am." If I were to put anything on the wall of my office, I would put a statement which says: BEING HERE IS NOT ENOUGH.

Thus the first task of analysis is very important: to help the patient be unhappy rather than to encourage him. In fact, any encouragement which tries to mitigate, to soften his suffering, is definitely not indicated; it is definitely bad for the further progress of the analysis. I don't think anyone has really enough initiative, enough impulse, to make the tremendous effort required by analysis—if we really mean analysis—unless he is aware of the maximum suffering which is in him. And that is not at all a bad state to be it. It's a much better state than to be in a shadowy land where one neither suffers nor is happy. Suffering is at least a very real feeling, and is a part of life. Not to be aware of suffering and to watch television or something is neither here nor there.

(b) Secondly, another condition is that the patient acquires or has *some idea of what his life ought to be*, or could be—some vision of what he wants. I have heard of patients who have come to an analyst because they couldn't write poetry. That's a little exceptional, although not so rare as one might think. But many patients come, because they are not happy. It's just not enough not to be happy. And if a patient were to tell me he wants to be analyzed because he is unhappy I would say: "Well, most people aren't happy." That isn't quite enough to spend years on a very energetic and troublesome and difficult work with one person.

To have an idea of what one wants in life is not a matter of education and also not a matter of cleverness. It might very well be that the patient never had a vision of his life. In spite of our overwhelming education systems people don't get in it many ideas of what they want in life. But nevertheless I think it is a task of the analysts also in the beginning of the analysis, to test whether the patient is capable of having some idea of what else life could mean except being happier. There are many words which patients in the big cities of the United States use: they want to express themselves, and all that—well, this is just phraseology. If somebody dabbles in music and likes hi-fi and this, that, or the other—these are just phrases. I think the analyst cannot be, must not be satisfied with these phrases, but must get down to reality: what is really the intention of this person—not theoretically—but what does he or she really want, what is he or she coming for.

(c) Another important factor is the *patient's seriousness.* You find many narcissistic people who go into analysis solely for the reason that they like to talk about themselves. In fact, where else can you do that? Neither one's wife nor one's friends nor one's children will listen by the hour to one's talking about oneself: what I did yesterday, and why I did it, and so on. Even the bartender will not listen that long because there are other customers. So one pays thirty-five dollars, or whatever the fee is, and one has a man who listens to my talking about myself all the time. Of course I have to catch on, as a patient, that I have to talk about psychologically relevant topics. So I must not talk about pictures and paintings and music; I must talk about myself, and why I didn't like my husband or my wife, and why I did like him or her, or what not. Now, that also must be excluded, because that is no sufficient reason for an analyst, although it's a good reason to make money.

(d) Another factor very closely related to this one is *the patient's capacity eventually to differentiate between banality and reality.* The conversation of most people, I think, is banal. The best example I could give of banality are the editorials of the New York Times, if you'll forgive me. What I mean by banality here, in contrast to reality, is not that something is not clever, but that it is unreal. If I read an article in the New York Times about the Vietnam situation, it is so banal to me. Of course it is a matter of political opinions—simply because it's unreal, because it deals with fictions, even to the degree that suddenly American ships fire at unseen targets and nobody knows what there was. And then all this has to do with the salvation from communism and God knows what. Well, this is banal. Similarly, the way people talk about their personal lives is banal, because they usually talk about unreal things: My husband did this or did that, or he got a promotion or he didn't get a promotion, and I should have called my boy friend or I shouldn't. . . . This is all banal because it doesn't touch upon anything real, it touches only upon rationalizations.

(e) Another factor is the *life circumstances of the patient.* How much neurosis he can successfully get by—that depends entirely on the situation. A salesman may get by with a form of neurosis with which a college professor might not get by. I don't mean because of a difference of cultural level, but simply because a certain type of highly narcissistic, aggressive behavior wouldn't do in a small college, they would throw him out. But if he's a salesman he may be extremely successful. Sometimes patients say: "Well, doctor, I just can't go on with that," and my standard answer to that gambit is: "Well, I don't see why you can't. You have gone on with it for 30 years and many people, millions of people go on with that until the end of their days, so why you can't I can't see. I could see why you wouldn't want to, but I need some proof why you don't want to or that you don't want to." But "You can't" is simply not true; that's also phraseology.

(f) The point which I want to stress most is the *active participation of the patient.* And here I come back to what I said before. I don't think anybody gets well by talking and not even by revealing his unconscious, just as little as anybody achieves anything of importance without making a very great effort and without making sacrifices, without risking, without going—if I could use symbolic language which often appears in dreams— through the many tunnels which one has to pass through in the course of life. That means periods when one finds oneself in the dark, periods where one is frightened, and yet where one has faith that there is another side of the tunnel, that there will be light. I think in this process the personality of the analyst is very important; namely, whether he is good company and whether he is able to do what a good mountain guide does, who doesn't carry his client up the mountain, but sometimes tells him:

"This is a better road," and sometimes even uses his hand to give him a little push, but that is all he can do.

(g) This brings me to the last point: the *personality of the analyst*. One could certainly give a lecture on that, but I just want to make a very few points. Freud already made one very important point, namely, the absence of sham and deception. There should be something in the analytic attitude and in the analytic atmosphere by which from the very first moment the patient experiences that this is a world which is different from the one he usually experiences: it's a world of reality, and that means a world of truth, truthfulness, without sham—that's all that reality is. Secondly, he should experience that he is not supposed to talk banalities, and that the analyst will call his attention to it, and that the analyst doesn't talk banalities, either. In order to do this, of course, the analyst must know the difference between banality and non-banality, and that is rather difficult, especially in the world in which we live.

Another very important condition for the analyst is the absence of sentimentality: one doesn't cure a sick person by being kind either in medicine or in psychotherapy. That may sound harsh to some, and I am sure I will be quoted for utter ruthlessness towards the patient, for lack of compassion and authoritarianism and what not. Well, that may be so. It's not my own experience of what I'm doing or my own experience with a patient, because there is something quite different from sentimentality, and that is one of the essential conditions to analyze: to experience in oneself what the patient is talking about. If I cannot experience in myself what it means to be schizophrenic or depressed or sadistic or narcissistic or frightened to death, even though I can experience that in smaller doses than the patients, then I just don't know what the patient is talking about. And if I don't make that attempt, then I think I'm not in touch with the patient.

There may be some people who have idiosyncrasies towards certain things. I remember Sullivan used to say that an anxiety-ridden patient never came to his office a second time because he just had no sympathy nor empathy for this kind of thing. Well, that's perfectly all right. Then one just doesn't take this kind of patient, and one is a very good therapist for those patients with whom one can feel what they feel.

It is a basic requirement of analysis to feel what the patient feels. That's the reason why there is no better analysis for analysts than analyzing other people, because in the process of analyzing other people there is almost nothing which is in the analyst that doesn't come up, that isn't touched, provided he or she tries to experience what the patient experiences. If he or she thinks: "Well, the patient is a poor sick guy because he pays," then of course he remains intellectual and he never is convincing to the patient.

The result of this attitude is that indeed one is not sentimental with a patient, but one is not lacking in compassion, because one has a deep feeling that nothing that happens to the patient is not also happening in oneself. There is no capacity to be judgmental or to be moralistic or to be indignant about the patient once one experiences what is happening to the patient as one's own. And if one doesn't experience this as one's own, then I don't think one understands it. In the natural sciences you can put the material on the table and there it is and you can see it and you can measure it. In the analytic situation it's not enough that the patient puts it on the table, because for me it's not a fact as long as I cannot see it in myself as something which is real.

Finally, it is very important to see the patient as the hero of a drama and not to see him as a summation of complexes. And, actually, every human being is the hero of a drama. I don't mean that in any sentimental fashion. Here is a person born with certain gifts, and usually he fails, and his life is a tremendous struggle to make something out of that which he is born with, fighting against tremendous handicaps. Even the most banal person in one sense, looking at it from the outside, is exceedingly interesting once you see him as that person, as that living substance which was thrown into the world at a place not desired by him nor known to him, and is fighting in some way his way through. Actually, the great writer is characterized precisely by the fact that he can show a person who is banal in one sense and yet who is a hero in the sense in which the artist sees him. Just to take one example, the figures of Balzac—most of them are not interesting and yet they become terribly interesting by the power of the artist. We are not Balzacs, so we cannot write these novels, but we should acquire the capacity of seeing in a patient a human drama, or, for that matter, in any human being in whom we are interested, and not just a person who comes with symptom A, B, C, D.

In concluding I want to say something about *prognosis*. I believe that in what I call the benign neuroses there is a very good chance of cure, in the malignant neuroses the chances are not very good. I won't go into percentages now because in the first place that is a professional secret or trade secret, and in the second place one would have to talk a lot about it. Nevertheless, I think it's a common experience that the chances for the cure of severe, malignant neuroses are not too good. I don't think there's anything to be ashamed about that. If you have in medicine a severe sickness and you have, let us say, a five percent chance of cure with a certain method—and I think the chances in analysis are even a little better—provided there is no better method and this is all that the physician can do, everybody—the physician, the patient, his friends, his relatives, everybody will make the greatest effort to achieve health, even though there is only a five percent chance. It is wrong not to see the difference between a benign neurosis and a malignant neurosis and to be in a kind of honeymoon mood in the beginning and to think: "Well, analysis cures everything." Or if the analyst tries in some way or another to kid himself, in looking at the patient, that things are not as severe and with as little hope as they sometimes are. Even in those cases in which a patient may not get well, at least one condition is fulfilled in a good analysis, and that is that the analytic hours, if they have been alive and significant, will have been the most important and the best hours that he ever had in his life. I think that cannot be said about many therapies, and that at least is a comfort to the analyst who struggles with patients who often have indeed a very low chance of cure.

In the non-malignant neuroses there is a much better chance. I would suggest to consider that among the light forms of neuroses many might be cured but by methods much shorter than two years of analysis; that is to say, by having the courage of using analytic insight to approach the problem very directly, and possibly to do in twenty hours what one feels obliged to do, as an analyst, in two hundred hours. There is no reason for false shame to use direct methods when they can be used.

Part II

Therapeutic Aspects of Psychoanalysis

· 4 ·

What Is Psychoanalysis?

The Aim of Psychoanalysis

The question with which I want to start is at the same time a basic question for all that follows: What is the aim of psychoanalysis? Now that's a very simple question and I think there's a very simple answer. To know oneself. Now this "To know oneself" is a very old, human need, from the Greeks to the Middle Ages to modern times you find the idea that knowing oneself is the basis of knowledge of the world or—as Meister Eckhart expressed it—in a very drastic form: "The only way of knowing God is to know oneself." This is one of the oldest human aspirations. And it is indeed an aspiration or an aim which has its roots in very objective factors.

How is one to know the world? How is one to live and react properly if the very instrument which is to act, which is to decide, is not known to ourselves? We are the guide, the leader of this "I" which manages in some way to live in the world, to make decisions, to have priorities, to have values. If this "I," this main subject which decides and acts, is not properly known to us, it must follow that all our actions, all our decisions are done half blindly or in a half-awakened state.

One has to think of the fact that man is not endowed with instincts like the animals, which tell him how to act so that he really does not have to know anything except what his instinct tells him. This requires a qualification, because even in the animal kingdom, the animal, and even the animal of a very low level of evolution, needs to learn something. Instincts do not operate without a minimum of learning at least. But that is only a minor point. By and large, the animal does not have to know much, although it has to have some experience which is indeed transmitted through memory.

But man has to know everything in order to decide. His instincts don't tell him anything about how to decide except that they tell him that he must eat, drink, defend himself, sleep, and possibly that he ought to produce children. The trick of nature is, you might say, to endow him with a certain pleasure or lust for sexual satisfaction. But that is not by far as strong an instinctive demand as the other drives or impulses are. So to know oneself is a condition not only from a spiritual or—if you like—religious, or moral, or human standpoint, it is a demand from the biological standpoint.

Because the optimum of efficiency in living depends on the degree to which we know ourselves as that instrument which has to orient itself in the world and make decisions. The better known we are to ourselves, obviously the more proper are the decisions we make. The less we know ourselves, the more confused must be the decisions we make.

Psychoanalysis is not only a therapy, but an instrument for self-understanding. That is to say an instrument for self-liberation, an instrument in the art of living, which is in my opinion the most important function psychoanalysis can have.

The main value of psychoanalysis is really to provide a spiritual change of a personality, and not to cure symptoms. As far as this is there to cure symptoms, that is fine if there are no better and shorter cures, but that the real historical importance of psychoanalysis goes in the direction of such knowledge which you find in Buddhist thinking. This kind of self-awareness—mindfulness—plays a central role in Buddhist practice to achieve a better state of being than the average man does.

Psychoanalysis claims that to know oneself leads to cure. Well, that's a claim which is made already in the Gospels: "The truth shall make you free." (John 8:32) Why does the knowledge of one's unconscious, that is to say full self-knowledge, help to make a person free from symptoms or make him even happy?

Sigmund Freud's Therapeutic Aim and My Critique on It

I first want to say a word about the therapeutic aims of classic, Freudian psychoanalysis. As Freud once put it, the therapeutic aim was to make a person capable of working and being able to function sexually. To put it in better, objective terms: the aim of psychoanalysis is to make a person capable of working and reproducing. These are indeed the two great demands of society, which society makes of everybody. It means to suggest, to indoctrinate people why they should work and why they should produce children. Well, we do it anyway for many reasons. The State doesn't have much trouble inducing people to do that, but if the State needs more children than are produced at any given moment, then it will do a great deal to get the desired number of children by all sorts of means.

Freud's definition of what is really mental health is essentially a social definition. It is to say to be normal in a social sense. Man shall function according to the socially patterned norms. Also the symptom is determined socially: A symptom is a symptom when it makes it difficult for you to function socially properly. Drug addiction, for instance, is considered a severe symptom. Compulsive smoking isn't. Why? It's the same thing, psychologically speaking. But the difference is very great, socially speaking. If you take certain kinds of drugs this prevents you from proper social functioning in many situations. You can smoke yourself to death—who cares? If you die from lung cancer, that's not a social problem. People will die anyway. But if you die from lung cancer when you are fifty—well, when you are fifty you are not socially important any more! Anyway you have produced the proper number of children, you have worked in the society, you have done your best; this is not interesting, this is not interfering with your social function.

We declare something a symptom when it is interfering with social function. That's why a person who is not capable of having the slightest bit of subjective experience and sees things only entirely realistically is supposed to be healthy. Although he is just as sick as a psychotic who cannot recognize reality as something manageable or as something to be manipulated, but he can recognize something here, a feeling, a most subtle feeling, an inner experience which is inaccessible to the so-called normal person.

The Freudian definition is essentially a social definition, and this is no critique in a narrower sense of the word because he was a man of his century and he never questioned his society. Freud never was critical of his society except that he felt the *tabu* on sex was too strong. It should be somewhat lowered. Freud himself was a very prudish man—exceedingly prudish—and he would have been certainly exceedingly shocked to see the kind of sexual behavior now which is allegedly the result of his teaching. In reality it isn't. Freud has little to do with that. The present sexual behavior is part of general consumerism.

How did Freud give reasons for the goals of psychoanalysis he set? To put it simply, according to Freud that which cures is related to an event in early childhood. This event is repressed. Because it is repressed it still operates. By the so-called *repetition compulsion* the person is bound to this early event in such a way that it does not only operate because of its inertia, because it is there, it has never ceased to work, but also because by the repetition compulsion the person is compelled to repeat the same pattern again and again. If this pattern is brought to consciousness then so to speak its energy is experienced fully, recalled but not only, as Freud soon saw, intellectually but affectively; if what he called *working through* happens—then the force of this trauma is broken and the person is free from this repressed influence.

I have grave doubts about the validity of this theory. First I want to tell you of a personal experience that I had when I was a student at the Psychoanalytic Institute in Berlin [from 1928 to 1930]. One day our professors had a long discussion—the students were usually present—how often it happens that a patient really remembers his early traumatic experiences. The majority of them said that was very rare. I was very startled; I was a good, faithful student; I believed in it and suddenly I hear that the very thing which is supposed to be the basis of cure happens so rarely. (Of course the professors had their way out. It was said that the trauma reappears in the transference—but I won't go into that now.)

The trauma in my opinion is indeed quite rare and it is indeed usually one single experience; it has to be really quite extraordinarily traumatic to have a strong effect. But many things which are said to be traumatic, namely that the father beat the boy once, at the age of three, when he was very furious—for Heaven's sake, that's not a traumatic event. That's a perfectly normal event because the influence is really constituted by the whole and continuous and constant atmosphere of the parents, of the family, and not by single events. Only rarely does a single event have such effects as it should have in the case of a real trauma. Today people talk of a real trauma because they missed the train or had some disagreeable experience somewhere. A trauma is by definition an event which goes beyond the charge which the human nervous circuit can tolerate. Since the person cannot tolerate the trauma, the trauma has created a deep disturbance. But most traumata in this sense are very rare and what is often called a trauma then is really all those things which happen in life and which have little influence. What has influence is a continuous atmosphere.

A trauma can occur at any age, but the same traumatic event will have a greater effect the earlier it happens. But in that case at the same time the recuperative powers of a child are also greater. It's really a complicated problem, and I'm only warning against the loose use of the word trauma, which is today I find very frequent.

I have seen quite a few people change through the analytic process. I have seen quite a few people not change. But there is also the fact that individuals have changed fundamentally without analysis. Take one simple thing which we have seen in the last two years. There are a number of people who were in their minds hawks about the war in Vietnam, conservative Air Force officers and so on. These people stay in Vietnam, they experience this, they see the senselessness, the injustice, the cruelty, and suddenly there comes something which one in older times would have called a conversion, namely suddenly these people see the world entirely differently and change from people who are in favor of the war to people who risk their lives or their freedom to stop the war. People you would not recognize, you could say that by themselves they are not different people, just by a striking experience, that by their own capacity to respond to it. This capacity is not given to most people because most people have become already too insensitive. But that deep changes do occur analytically and outside of analysis, I think for that we have pretty much evidence. It can be seen again and again.

Freud's Concept of the Child and My Critique on It

Freud was exceedingly critical, as everybody knows who has read a little of Freud, with regard to his specific theme namely of conscious thought in relationship to unconscious motivation. Freud could certainly not be accused of not having been a radical critic of conscious thought. Yet when it comes to the society in which he lived, and its rules and its values, Freud was basically reformist. That is to say he took the same attitude which the liberal middle class took in general: Basically this is the best of all worlds, but it could be improved. It could be improved, maybe we could have longer periods of peace, prisoners could be treated better. The middle class never asked radical questions, for instance the question of criminology. Our whole system of criminology, of punishing, is entirely based on the class structure. They never asked: Is not the criminal primarily a man who is a criminal because this is his way of finding an optimum of satisfaction which he cannot get any other way? I don't want to defend here thieves and robbers. I think there is another dimension which makes thieving and robbing quite unpleasant. But nevertheless, our whole system of criminal law is based on the whole structure of society which takes it for granted that the vast majority is—as one says politely—underprivileged, or more honestly, that the minority is overprivileged. This was also the case in the not radical pacifism with the reduction of armies; treaties should ensure peace.

And so psychoanalysis was a movement to make a better life by some reforms in consciousness. But it did not question radically the value and the structure of existing society. With his sympathies Freud was on the side of those who dominated—of the establishment. Well, you can see that in Freud's attitude to the First World War. He believed until 1917 that the Germans would win. That was the year when most people who had some knowledge had already gotten over their beliefs that the Germans would win. I think of one letter Freud wrote: "I am so happy to be in Hamburg, to be able to say: 'Our soldiers, our victories,'" because it was in Germany. Today that really sounds frightful. One has to understand the fantastic effect, the signal effect on the conscience of even the most intelligent and otherwise decent people in the First World War.

You can only understand this if you compare that with Vietnam at its worst. There was almost no opposition to the war in the First World War, and that was one of the tragedies about it. Einstein was one of the few exceptions who refused to endorse the war, but the vast majority of German intellectuals or French intellectuals approved of the war. And so Freud's statement is not that unusual, not that strong as it may sound outside of context, but nevertheless it is pretty strong if you consider that it was that late. And it was written by men like Freud who in 1925, in his letter exchanged with Einstein, called himself a "pacifist."

How did Freud see the child? Originally when Freud heard the reports of patients that they had been seduced by their parents, girls by their fathers and boys by their mothers, he believed that these were reports of real events. And for all I know that was probably so. Ferenczi at the end of his life believed the same. But Freud very soon changed his viewpoint and said: No, these were all fantasies. The parents couldn't, the parents didn't do that, that wasn't true. The children of these people then told these stories because they talked about their own fantasies. They had this incestuous fantasy of sleeping with father, or with mother, or whatever the case may be. And all these stories are a proof for the incestuous semi-criminal fantasy of the young child.

As you know, this forms the rock bottom of psychoanalytic theory, namely the theory that the child, the infant already is filled with—as Freud called it—polymorphous-perverse fantasies. Freud really meant something pretty bad, that this child is a greedy child who can think of nothing else but how to seduce her father or his mother—and with a wish to sleep with them. That, of course, slanted the whole psychoanalytic viewpoint in a wrong direction. First of all, it led to the theoretical assumption that these incestuous fantasies were an essential part of a child's equipment. Secondly, that in analyzing a person you must always assume that everything of this kind which a patient reports is due to his own fantasy and needs to be analyzed and does not represent reality.

Basically, Freud's principle was: the child is "guilty" and not the parents. And this comes through very clearly in Freud's own case histories. Together with some colleagues, I have shown it in the "Comments on 'The Case of Little Hans'" (E. Fromm et al., 1966k): The parents, even those who are most obvious, selfish, antagonistic, hostile, are always defended by Freud. The onus, the charge is always on the child. This child with these incestuous fantasies (and not only incestuous; then of course the child wanted to murder the father, to rape the mother), this child was, as Freud himself said, a "mini-criminal."

This picture of the child as a "mini-criminal" one must understand dynamically as a consequence of the need to defend parental authority: to defend authority and thus defend the parents. If you go through the life of most children, then indeed you will find that parental love is one of the greatest fictions that have ever been invented. Usually parental love masks—as Laing has said quite correctly—the power the parent wants to have over the child. I don't mean that there are not exceptions. There are real exceptions, there are some loving parents, I have seen some. But on the whole, if you read the history of the treatment of children by their parents through the ages, and if you see the history of people today, then you will find that indeed the main interest of most parents is control of the children, and that what their love is I would call a kind of sadistic level: "I mean your best, and I love you inasmuch as you don't try to rebel against my control."

It is a love which you had in the patriarchal society, of the father, of the husband to the wife; children have been property since the days of Rome and are still property. Still a parent has the absolute right to dispose of his child. There are a few attempts in various countries now to change this and to appoint a court, which could take away the right of a parent to bring up the child if there is some serious reason to believe he is incompetent to bring up the child. This is all so much eyewash, because until a court decides that parents are incompetent, the judges are parents themselves and are just as incompetent—so how could they decide that? Aside from the rather semi-instinctive and somewhat narcissistic love of mothers for their infants, up to the age when they show the first signs of their own will, from then on the tendency to control and to possess is dominating. For most people, their own sense of power, of control, of having importance, of moving something, of the feeling that they have something to say is by having children. Therefore—what I am saying is no malicious picture of parents, it's very natural. You see, the British upper class by and large didn't give a damn about their children. The upper classes in Europe had their gouvernantes, their governesses and so on; the mothers didn't care a hoot about their children, because there were plenty of other satisfactions in life. They were having their love affairs, they were having their parties, they were interested—in England—in their horses, and so on.

Children are looked at as possession as long as in people the wish to have is the dominant quality of their character structure. There are people in whom this wish to have is not dominant, but they are very rare today. So it is quite natural; children are so accustomed to take that for granted because the whole society says that's natural. The consensus is from the Bible on: The Bible says a rebellious son must be stoned and killed. Well, we don't do that anymore, but what happened to a rebellious son in the 19th century was quite strong.

If you analyze parental love, I would say, by and large, it's a human faculty, it's something very understandable, something with which one can feel great empathy and even sorrow and compassion, if you like. But nevertheless it is essentially in most people at best benign possessive and a tremendous number of malignant possessive, that is to say beating, hurting—and hurting in the many ways in which people are not even aware that they are hurting, hurting in the sense of dignity: hurting the sense of pride, making the child which is so sensitive and at the same time so intelligent, feel he is a nincompoop, he is stupid, he doesn't understand. Even some of the most well-meaning people do that, exhibit their children as if they were little clowns in front of other people. Everything under the sun is done to make a child feel inferior, to depress the state of self-confidence, of dignity, of freedom in a child.

The affirmation, this conformity of Freud with the dominant class, with his establishment, really did a great deal to distort his theory about children, and did a great deal to distort his therapy, because the analyst made himself the defender of the parents. But I think the analyst should be the accuser of the parents. An analyst should have an objective view. But if he is the defender of the parents because that is the spirit of the establishment, then he will not do much good to the patient. To be more accurate I should go a step further, adding one should not see just the whole family system but the whole social system, because the family is only a segment, is only a paradigm.

When I said for Freud the child is guilty I didn't mean the child is always innocent and I didn't mean the parents are always guilty; I think in each case it is a matter of a total study to what extent the child also contributes to the reaction of the parents. For instance, some parents are just allergic to a certain type of children. Let us say a very sensitive mother, somebody who is a little shy, gets a boy who is aggressive, a little crude—and you can see that also at the age of eight weeks: that's his temperament with which he is born. And she can't stand that child, she could never, she couldn't stand a person later on with his qualities. Well, that's just too bad. Because, you might say, he is not to be blamed, he is born the way he is and the mother is not to be blamed either, because she can't help it.

There are children which are born terrible, there are some very arrogant. Freud was such a little boy; he was terribly arrogant towards his father. He wetted his bed and said to his father: "When I am grown up I'll buy you the nicest bed in the town." It didn't occur to him to be sorry and apologize, as most children would do, but he was so sure of himself. Well, to some fathers this would make a boy intolerable, this kind of arrogance. In other words, the child contributes already some to the parents' reaction by his own being, and it is just a fiction to assume that it's one's own child, therefore it would be born as a child which is sympathetic to one. After all, it is the lottery of genes which plays here, and one doesn't always win in the lottery. And besides that, the child in the process also does many things which go beyond that, for which one can make the parents responsible.

The Relevance of Childhood Experiences for the Therapeutic Process

I am convinced that a great deal happens in the first five years which really are very important for the development of the person, but I think many other things happen later which are equally important and may change things.

For Freud, really, the concept of repetition compulsion—that the main things happen in the first five years and then things are just repeated—that to me is too mechanistic a concept. I think nothing in life is repeated, only mechanical things can be repeated. And in all sorts of things which happen, things change, although I would put—if I could say that in parenthesis—a good deal of emphasis on the constitutional factor. Freud did that theoretically, he said so, but I think most analysts, and especially the public, think that what a person becomes is in fact a result of what his parents did to him. And then they get to this kind of sob story which you find so often in analysis: "My father didn't love me, my mother didn't love me, my grandmother didn't love me and so I am a nasty person." Well, that is very easy, so you give all the fault to the people around.

In everybody's development you can demonstrate that there are certain elements in childhood which already lay the ground for later; but it is also a fact that later events either increase or fortify or weaken these elements. So you cannot say later events do not contribute. I look at this problem in that way that early events do not *determine* a person but they *incline* him. That is to say nothing that has happened earlier, I believe, necessarily determines a person but it inclines him, and the longer he goes on in this direction the more he is inclined, until you might say only by a miracle a change could still occur.

It is the aim of psychoanalysis to arrive at an insight into the unconscious processes which the patient has right now. Psychoanalysis is not historical research per se. We want to know, we want to take an x-ray of what goes on in the patient unconsciously now, that is to say behind his own back. That is our aim. Very often, however, the patient himself will understand this only if he can experience some re-experience, some childhood experiences, because they will really give flavor or specificity to something right now which he is not aware of. Sometimes that happens in transference, sometimes it happens in remembering something which he experienced as a child or even which he experienced in our session—we are full of these experiences. Sometimes it comes up in a dream.

It happens that something comes up in a dream which happens thirty years ago, when the patient was seventeen. But my aim is not historical research. My aim is the clearest awareness of that which is unconscious now, but in order to reach that aim very often, maybe most of the time, it is necessary to see what the patient experienced when he was a child, when he was an adolescent. Actually, when I am analyzing myself, which I do every day, I try quite intentionally to feel what I felt about this or the other when I was five, when I was fifteen; I try to see what of these feelings is in me. I try to constantly keep open my own connection with my childhood, to keep it alive, because it helps me to recognize and to be aware of things which go on in me now and which I am not aware of. The aim is not historical research.

Freud's idea was that if you bring to consciousness, and not only to intellectual but to eventually affective consciousness, very important experiences of childhood—pathogenic experiences of childhood—then by this process the symptom disappears, to put it very briefly. What has become of that? In a great deal of psychoanalysis and in the mind of the public [...] is what you might call a Freudian genetic explanation. I have heard so many stories of people whom one asks: "So, what has your analysis shown?" and then the formula, the logic is: "I am, this, this, or this, or have this or that symptom because..."—that is to say a *causal* explanation of a genetic historical nature. That in itself, of course, has no curative value whatsoever. If you know *why* something's happened, then that by itself does not change anything.

I want to call your attention to one thing, which is perhaps not entirely easy to understand: the difference between experiencing something in me, which was repressed and which suddenly comes up to my awareness, and on the other hand making these historical constructions because this and that happened. Because it is so rare that one finds these original experiences and that they are in a true sense recalled, one is often satisfied with a construction: It must have happened, it probably did happen, and because it did happen, you are this, that, and the other. One might call this approach useless. "If somebody drowns and knows about the laws of gravity, he drowns just the same [...]."

The childhood experience is of importance only insofar as it is re-experience, as it is recalled. In a second way, the knowledge of childhood helps to an easier understanding of what goes on now because one can, on theoretic grounds, make some assumptions about these childhood conditions and what we might expect.

What matters really is not the historical genetic approach, but what I call the x-ray approach. What matters are the forces driving me or motivating me or somebody else at this very moment, as if I took an x-ray—and that's why I use this analogy—to see what I cannot see under normal conditions of vision. If, for instance, you take a chest x-ray, you see also tuberculosis which a person may have had twenty years before; it shows in the scars of the tissue. But you are not interested in what he had twenty years before, you are interested to see what goes on now in the lungs of this person. Is there an active process that can be seen by the x-ray? If you want to understand something by analysis or by yourself without benefit of analysis, the point is always primarily to ask yourself what goes on now unconsciously, what can I surmise, what can I sense of unconscious motivations which determine me, and not what *went* on by which I can explain what goes on now.

Therapeutic Practice and the Relevance of Psychoanalysis

Freudian theory is, as you know, essentially an instinctivistic one; that is to say everything is based on the instinct and, of course, then how the environment has biased the instincts from the character. So in theory the psychoanalysts could almost be called on the side of instinctivism. In practice the psychoanalysts—also the Freudians—you might say are really environmentalists. They really follow roughly a simple principle: every child is what the parents have made of it. It is really completely the influence of their environment which determines the fate of a person and not what Freud calls the "constitutional factors." Freud himself has been much more careful than these. He has said constitutional factors—that is to say what we are born with, our hereditary factors—and environmental factors are a continuum in which the weight of each factor differs from case to case. You find persons in which the constitutional factor is much more powerful, and others in which the environmental factor is more powerful, but it is a continuum. On the one end, you would have the constitution, and on the other end you would have the environment.

In the practice of psychoanalysis—and I think of the American public here—there is a simple equation which leaves out the constitutional factors, where everything is the result of environment. And so, of course, it is also said that parents are responsible for everything that has happened. Now, they are in a way, but in another way they are not *that* responsible, because the result is that today mothers who have attended lectures in psychoanalysis are afraid of kissing their children or their sons because they produce an Oedipus complex, and they are afraid of ever having a firm opinion because they are authoritarian and that will cause a neurosis.

On the other hand, people who are analyzed live in the happy feeling that they are responsible for nothing, because they are just what their parents made them to be—it's too bad— and there's nothing they can do about it except go into psychoanalysis, and then you talk a lot about what your parents did to you, which doesn't make you change either, necessarily.

In reality, there is a constant interaction between the parents and the constitution of a person and how the person reacts to what parents do. The child at five, at four, already has his own reactions, therefore one cannot simply say: "I am this way because my mother was this way." Surely my mother or my father or my environment were the prime determining influences, but at the same time one has to ask oneself, what did I do, not to succumb to these influences? Was I completely a piece of wax, was I completely an empty piece of paper upon which my parents wrote their text? Did I not have as a child some possibility of deciding differently? Was I without any will? Am I completely determined by the circumstances?

In fact, in that way the popular concept of psychoanalysis is pretty much identical with Skinnerianism. It really amounts to saying they are conditioned that way and that's why they are that way. Only Skinner doesn't take the trouble to find out what is in the black box, what is inside of this person which transmits the conditioning factor to the result, to the behavior of the person. He is not interested in that; he is not interested in many things anyway which are not pure manipulation of people. But if you add this theoretical viewpoint, of the Freudian school, then it amounts to saying: "Well, we are conditioned that way, and well, you could describe the analytic process of the Skinnerian standpoint then as a great attempt of deconditioning." The mother has said: "I love you if you don't leave me" and the analyst says: "You are a good patient if you leave her." If that goes on for a few years, you accept another set of conditioning which might eventually get the patient to leave his mother and cleave to his analyst, and then you have the long-drawn-out so-called transference, and if then eventually there is no more pretext to continue the analysis, you cleave to some other person.

Many people marry, go from their mother to their wives, and that becomes a substitute, or they choose some other mother figure or authority figure, and that's what makes politics work, these allegiances which are created, in which people need the figure on which they are dependent. The only thing they don't do is to make themselves independent, but rather change dependencies. That is a great problem, but not only in Freudian therapy; it is a problem which you find in all analytic therapy.

This kind of emphasis on the conditioning factors which have made people the way they are lead more and more to neglect the real and important questions. These are: what could people do to extricate themselves? How they could act differently? How they could have made use of that margin of freedom which everyone has? And the crucial question, of course, what they could do now. This question is not dependent on age. One of my older patients was a woman of seventy who has really changed her whole life as a result of the analysis. But she was very alive; she was more alive than most people are at twenty.

Freud had a concept in which at least constitutional factors—that is to say, that which is in a person—played a role. A great deal of psychoanalysis today has deteriorated into a pure conditioning therapy—in fact, not in theory—and with no emphasis on the responsibility of the person involved. The question: "Why am I the way I am?" is about the basic formula for most psychotherapy, while I aim to see: "Who am I?" and not "Why am I the way I am?" My way of questioning I call taking a x-ray of oneself, because if you don't now why you are the way you are, you never know who you are.

Harry Stack Sullivan's Contribution to the Psychoanalytic Concept of Man

Sullivan started out his work very interestingly and convincingly. He was working in St. Elizabeth hospital in Washington and he asked to be permitted to make an experiment. He wanted to have a ward for his own patients, and—that was a condition—in this ward he would have only nurses who were selected and who were instructed and who would behave in a human way to the patients. At that time there was no psychotherapy, of course no drugs, and he did not do anything with the patients except exhibit his own personality, which was one of tremendous respect for psychotic patients, and a different behavior. The rate of spontaneous cures showed a remarkable change. That these patients were not mistreated, were not humiliated, were treated as human beings, had the effect that they got well. This is *prima facie* evidence that a psychosis is not just a physical, organic happening. A psychological change of this order can produce a cure in a patient who, in State hospital, would deteriorate and become a chronic psychotic at that time.

The importance of Sullivan lies theoretically in the recognition that what is important is not the libido, the sexual instinct, but really the personal relationship of one person to another—what he called "interpersonal relations." While Freud had thought the center of the problem was sexual attraction of the child, that is to say the so-called Oedipus complex, Sullivan and his people did not think that this was the main problem at all; in fact that was not a problem. The problem was what was pathological, what was peculiar in the personal relationships in a family which can generate schizophrenia. There are a number of studies outside of Sullivan too, brilliant studies to show what the schizogenic family is really like, and one has found—especially Laing , but others also—that a schizogenic family, the family which produces schizophrenics, is not a particularly vicious family. It's not a family in which the child is particularly mistreated. It is a family of absolute boredom, of absolute emptiness, of lifelessness, of no genuine relation of anyone to the other, which starves a child in his need for personal contact.

Strengthened by animal experiments everybody knows today, evidence suggests that if a child does not have an early physical contact with the mother or a mother substitute, this creates great damage for further development. It's a vital need for the child. Everybody knows and accepts that, but what many people forget is that the need to have this kind of interpersonal stimulation is equally great and lasts much longer than this original need for physical contact with the mother. If it isn't there, the child does not die like the children which René Spitz describes—it's doesn't make that deep physiological impact—but if it's particularly severe, the child becomes so brittle, so schizoid, so unrelated that when there is a certain amount of tension it breaks down and becomes a manifest schizophrenic.

Sullivan was the first therapist who tried to create a theory of schizophrenia which basically believed that schizophrenia was not essentially an organic illness but was essentially a result of a psychological process. This was, of course, one of the greatest changes from Freudian theory, because Freud had declared that the psychotic cannot be helped, the psychotic could not be analyzed. In his view it was because he was so narcissistic that he would not get into this transference relation with the therapist. I still think one can define a psychotic person as a person with an extremely high degree of narcissism, that is to say, for whom only that which is inside of him is real— that which pertains to his own ideas, to his own personality— and nothing is real that pertains to the outside world. But at the same time a schizophrenic patient is often an extremely sensitive person and is in fact also quite capable of responding to people. However, people must be more sensitive than the average person is, and then the schizophrenic will react; he will respond. In many instances, even severely catatonic patients know what goes on and respond in their peculiar way, and can tell you later, when they are out of it, what they had experienced; and how they had understood what was going on.

Sullivan and this whole tradition is a very important new aspect of psychoanalysis, which for the first time gave the psychotic person the dignity of a full-fledged human being. It was, after all, only during the French Revolution that one had freed psychotic patients from their chains, and if you were to see some State hospitals even today, they are not chained, but still it isn't much better. The psychotic is still looked upon— also I would say by most conventional psychiatrists, as a nut, as a person entirely different, as somebody over there, and few psychiatrists have the capacity to sense that something of the schizophrenic is in every one of us. Just as something of a manic-depressed person is in every one of us. And certainly there is something of a paranoid person in any one of us. We are all in parts—paranoia is a state which is only a matter of degree. Up to a certain point we call it normal, and if we can't stand it we call it sickness. So none of these psychotic states are really so different, create such deep gaps between human beings. And a psychotic patient is not inhuman, dehumanized, different from the so-called normal patient.

Diseases of Our Time as Challenge to Psychoanalysis

Traditionally psychoanalysis is understood as essentially a therapeutic process of people who are sick. If I have a compulsion to doubt everything, an obsessional doubt, if I have a paralyzed arm psychogenetically, that is a solid symptom. Psychoanalysis is not the only method by which one can cure symptoms. I have been in Lourdes and I have seen many people who have been cured from paralysis and all sorts of severe symptoms by their faith in Lourdes. People really get cured, without any doubt. People today get cured by the many methods which are announced; there are all sorts of names, and if it's a matter of getting cured, then many of those methods are good.

You can cure people also by terror. In the First World War a German physician made an invention to heal soldiers who were shell-shocked out of fright and panic; the cure he used was to put their bodies under a strong electric current, which apparently really hurts, very deeply. His name was Dr. Kaufmann, and it was the Kaufmann treatment. That was medical, that was to cure. It was pure torture, and it turned out that the fear of this torture was greater than the fear and panic of being in the trenches again. And so, by this terror system, people were cured from a symptom. What it did to the person to have one terror driven out by a greater terror is, of course, a question in which Dr. Kaufman and the army in general had no particular interest.

But many symptoms can be cured also and perhaps exclusively by psychoanalysis, namely certain cases of obsessional doubts, of all kinds of obsessional symptoms, of certain hysterical symptoms. Sometimes it's very easy. Let me give you an example of a very easy, very simple analytic treatment which took only a few hours for curing a symptom. I remember a woman who came to me with a complaint, with a symptom: whenever she left her home, she had the obsessional idea that she had left the gas on or that for some other reason there would be a fire; and wherever she was, she had a compulsion to go back to her home and to see that there was no fire. That actually sounds mild when one talks about it, but it was completely destructive to her whole life because she practically couldn't go out. She had to run back, and it was unconquerable, this symptom. Then she talked about her past. She mentioned that she had been operated on for cancer about four or five years earlier and the not-too-sensitive surgeon had told her that of course while the danger was removed for the moment, there could be metastasis and cancer could spread like fire. That was, of course, a very frightening prospect—it would be for anybody to be told this—and she was terribly frightened of the spread of cancer. She succeeded in translating the fear that the cancer would spread to the fear that fire would spread. So she was not afraid of cancer, she was afraid of fire, and while this was disruptive, the symptom itself was a cure of a worse fear, the fear of getting cancer.

It happened that at that moment—as I said it was about five years after her operation—the chances of a recurrence of a metastasis were relatively small and so at that point she lost her fear of fire without being afraid of cancer anymore. But if you think of a year, three years earlier, then it would have been doubtful whether one did her any good to know her fear of fire, because then, if she became conscious of this, her fear of cancer would have recurred and that would have been much more painful and much more disturbing than her fear of fire. Here you have a very simple symptom, about the simplest one you could find, which can disappear almost immediately when it's translated and connected to what the person is really afraid of. Now most cases are more complicated, but I would say by and large in instances where analysis is used for this therapy of symptoms analysis is enough.

At the time of Freud most people who came to a psychiatrist suffered from such symptoms, especially from hysterical symptoms, which today are very rare. It's a change, you can see here, a change in the style of neurosis which goes together with the change of cultural patterns. Hysteria is a great outburst of feeling and if you see an hysterical person with all this outburst of emotion and shouting and crying and all this, then you may think at the same time of the orator of the last century, of the love-letters and so on—all these things if we see them in the movies today sound plain funny. It is because we have a completely different style. We have a matter-of-fact style, we don't show much feeling, and today schizoid symptoms, symptoms of lack of connectedness with other people and their results, are the frequent symptoms.

At the time of Freud people suffered in the first line of symptoms—not only hysterics, of course, but also compulsive symptoms. At that time people who had a real massive-symptom illness, which they could prove by having symptoms, went to a psychiatrist. Today I would say most people who go to a psychoanalyst are people who suffer from what he used to call "la malaise du siécle," the uneasiness which is characteristic for our century. No symptoms at all, but feeling unhappy, strange, not even sleeplessness, life has no meaning, no zest of life, drifting, a feeling of vague malaise. And they expect that analysis may change that. One calls that character analysis, the analysis of the whole character, rather than symptom analysis, because you might say indeed that there are people who suffer from this malaise, which one cannot define very properly in words but which one can feel very precisely from looking into oneself and into other people.

One has called this type of psychoanalysis *character analysis* which is a somewhat more scientific name or word for *people who suffer from themselves*. There is nothing wrong. They have everything but they suffer from themselves. And they don't know what to do with themselves, they suffer from it, it's a burden, it's a task which they cannot solve. It's a puzzle; they can solve a crossword puzzle but they cannot solve the puzzle which life offers to everyone.

For this type of malaise psychoanalysis in the classic sense, in my opinion, is not enough. A different type is needed because this malaise amounts to the question of a radical change in the whole personality. Nobody who suffers from the malaise can be successfully analyzed without a radical change and without a transformation of his character. Small changes and small improvements do not do any good. Modern systems theory can clarify this. I am referring to the concept that a personality—or an organization—is a system. That is to say it's not just a sum total of many parts, but it is a structure. If one part of the structure is changed it touches upon all other parts. The structure in itself has a cohesion; it tends to reject changes because this structure itself tends to retain itself.

If one makes in this structure small changes, it doesn't change much. To give a simple example: The idea was common to change the situation in a slum by building better houses in the slum. What happens? After three or five years, the nice new houses are exactly the same as the slum houses. Why? Because the education has remained the same, income has remained the same, health has remained the same, the cultural patterns have remained the same—that is to say, the whole system grows over this little change, this little oasis, and after a while it is incorporated again into the whole system. You could change the slum only if you change the whole system—change at the same time the income, the education, health, the lives of people completely. Then you will change also the houses. But if you change one part that is not enough. That cannot resist the impact of the system which is—so to speak—interested in its own survival of the system. [...]

In the same sense an individual is a system or a structure. If you try to make little changes you will soon find that after a while these new changes disappear, that nothing has really changed and that only a very basic transformation of your personality system will in the long run produce a change. That would comprise your thinking, your acting, your feeling, your moving, everything. And even one step which is integrated, which is total, is more affective than ten steps which are only in one direction. You see the very same thing in social change, where also one change never produces a lasting effect.

· 5 ·

Preconditions for Therapeutic Cure

The Ability for Psychic Growth

If we think of today's widespread character neuroses, then we have to ask a question: Why is it that a person develops in what we call a neurotic, unhappy way? Why is it that he isn't as he wants to be, that he has so little happiness in life?

I would suggest one consideration which is a result of my observation in life, that there is a general law that every human being, like every animal, like every seed, wants to live and wants to have an optimum of pleasure, satisfaction out of life. Nobody wants to be unhappy. Not a masochist either; for him masochism is the particular way in which he gets an optimum of pleasure. The reason people are healthier or less healthy or suffer more or suffer less lies in the fact that, due to their circumstances, their errors, the misdirection of their lives (which is systematic from the third year on), and also some-times constitutional factors and the particular combination of circumstances, they do not have the proper conditions for having the maximum of development which a human person could have. So they seek their own salvation in a crippled way.

I want to compare the crippled potentialities of psychic growth with a tree in the garden; it's between two walls in a corner and has little sun. This tree has grown completely crooked, but it has grown that way because it was its only way to get to the sun. If you would speak about a man you might say this tree is a vicious crippled man because he is really thoroughly crooked. He is not at all as he should be, according to his potentialities. But why is he that way? Because this was his only way to get light. This is what I mean here. Everybody tries to get to the sun to get an increase in life. But if the circumstances are such that he cannot get it in a more positive way, then he will get it in a crooked way. By "crooked" I mean it here symbolically, in a sick way, in a distorted way. And yet he is still a human being, trying his best to find a solution to his life. That one should never forget.

If you see a person with the above mentioned malaise, then one also should never forget that this person has developed in this way because he is still looking for a solution to his life. He is eager to find it. But there are many circumstances which make it extremely difficult for him and which may make him even resist, because he is too frightened of any attempt to help him to change his course.

It is an exceedingly difficult task to change oneself and to achieve a real—you might say—transformation of character. In fact this has been the aim of all religions, and of most philosophies. Certainly it was the aim of Greek philosophy and the aim of some modern philosophies, and it doesn't matter whether you speak of Buddhism or whether you speak of Christianity or Judaism or of Spinoza or Aristotle. They all have tried to find out what man can do to give himself instructions, to lead himself to a better, higher, healthier, more joyful way, a more forceful way of living. Most people act out of duty because they feel they owe: that means they are dependent. They have not yet reached the point of their self-affirmation, of their putting themselves "This is me, this is my life, this is my conviction, this is my feeling, and I act according to—not to my whims—this would be irrational—but according to what one could call the rational manifestation of myself or, you might say, the essential requirements or essential powers of my personality—"essential" meaning here that which belongs to the essence of myself as man. As against, too, those drives which are irrational.

What does it mean to be "rational"? Whitehead (1967, p. 4) said, "the function of reason is to promote the art of living." If I would put it in my own words I would say: Rational is all that, all actions and all behavior, which furthers the growth and development of a structure. Irrational are all such acts of behavior which slow down or destroy the growth and structure of an entity, whether that is a plant or whether that is a man. These things, according to the Darwinian theory, have developed in the sense of being a safe part of the interests of survival of the individual and of the species. Hence basically they further the interests of the individual and of the species and therefore they are rational. Sexuality is perfectly rational. Hunger and thirst are perfectly rational.

The trouble with man is that he is very little determined by instincts. Otherwise if man were an animal he would be perfectly rational—every animal is perfectly rational—if you lose your habit of thought to confuse rational with intellectual. Rational does not mean something necessarily which is thought; rational really refers just as much to an action. To give an example: If somebody puts a factory in a place where labor is scarce and expensive and he needs much more labor than machinery, then he acts economically irrationally because his action is bound to weaken and eventually destroy his economic system, the system of this plant, and he will soon notice it when after a year or two he is bankrupt.

Since Frederick Winslow Taylor, economists are speaking of "rationalization" in an entirely different sense from our psychological rationalization. Rationalization means to change the methods of work in such a way that they are more adequate from the standpoint of the optimal functioning of this economic unit—not from the standpoint of man.

According to man one has to say: His instincts are not irrational, but his passions are. The animal has no envy, no destructiveness for its own sake, no wish to exploit, no sadism, no wish to control, all these are passions which are by and large hardly present at all in the mammals. In man they develop not because they are rooted in his instincts, but because they are produced by certain pathological conditions in his environment which produce pathological traits in man. To give a simple example: If you have a seed of a rose bush, you know that for this seed to produce a full grown bush with beautiful roses it needs exactly that much moisture, temperature, a special kind of earth, to be planted at a certain time. If these conditions are given, this seed will—short of the plague or other outstanding, special circumstances—develop into a perfect rose. If you put a seed into a soil which is terribly moist, it will just decay, the seed will perish. If you put it under conditions which are not optimal conditions, then you will have a rose bush, but the rose bush will show defects in its growth, in its flowers, in its leaves and everything. Because the seed of the rose bush was meant to develop fully only if those conditions are given which are empirically—and that is only to be found out empirically—conducive to the growth of this particular seed.

This holds true also for an animal, as any animal breeder knows, and that holds true for man, too. We know that man for his full growth needs certain conditions. If these conditions are not given, if instead of warmth there is coldness, if instead of freedom there is coercion, if instead of respect there is sadism, then the child will not die but he will become a warped child, just as we have a warped tree when it doesn't get any sun, which it needs. These passions, which are the warped passions, which are the result of inadequate conditions—these are the irrational passions of man. And of them it can be said they are not furthering the inner system of man, but they tend to weaken it, or they eventually destroy it, sometimes even in illness.

The Individual's Responsibility for Psychic Growth

Freud brought the final breakthrough of a process which lasted for centuries: the unmasking of thought by the knowledge that honesty is not defined by proving that one consciously has good intentions—for somebody can lie with the best intentions or with the feeling that he is completely sincere, because his lies are not conscious. By that, Freud gave an entirely new dimension to the problem of honesty, of sincerity, in human relations, because the excuse "I didn't mean it"—which is the traditional excuse for not intending what an act seems to indicate—has really lost its significance since Freud's theory of slips of the tongue and other events.

Since Freud the moral problem also has to be reconsidered: A person is responsible not only for what he thinks but for his own unconscious. This is where responsibility begins, the rest is mask, the rest is nothing; what a person believes is hardly worth listening to. I am saying this with slight exaggeration: you will find many speeches and many assurances and many utterances which are hardly worth listening to because you know that it is all part of the pattern, of the picture someone wants to present.

For therapy, in my view, the important thing is that the patient can mobilize his or her own sense of responsibility and activity. I think a good deal of what goes on under analysis today is based on an assumption which many patients have: that this is a method in which one gets happy by talking without taking risks, without suffering, without being active, without making decisions. This doesn't happen in life and it doesn't happen in analysis. Nobody gets happy by talking, not even by talking in order to get interpretations.

In order to change, the patient must have a tremendous will and impulse to change. Everybody blames somebody and he thereby evades responsibility. If I say responsibility, I am not talking from the standpoint of a judge. I do not accuse anyone.

I do not think we have a right to accuse anyone as if we were judges. But still this is a fact: Nobody gets well unless he has an increasing sense of responsibility, of participation, and in fact a sense of pride in his achievement of getting well.

There are certain conditions which are conducive to healthy development of man and certain conditions which are conducive to pathological phenomena, and the crucial question is to find out what are the conditions which are conducive to the healthy development of man and what are the pathogenic conditions. And in fact what are the conditions which are conducive to the healthy development of man is a topic which has usually been treated under the category of ethics in the history of thought. Because ethics is essentially the attempt to show those norms which are conducive to the healthy development of man.

As soon as one talks about men, people say it's a value judgment because they don't want to think about norms which are necessary: they want to live happily without knowing how to live happily. As Meister Eckhart once said: "How can man learn the art of living and of dying without any instruction?" That is perfectly true and it's perfectly crucial. Today people think they can become very happy.They have all the dreams of happiness, but they have not the slightest idea what conditions are conducive to happiness, nor to any kind of satisfactory life.

I have a distinct ethical conviction and a model about how a culture would be that is conducive to well-being. Not that I could give an exact blueprint of how that society would look specifically, because that's very difficult, practically impossible to do, because in new circumstances new things arise in detail, thus also our knowledge changes and in some ways increases every day. But nevertheless about the ethical model I have the distinct conviction: In such a culture the main purpose of life is the *full development of man* and not things and not production, not wealth, not riches. In which the process of living itself, if you please, is a work of art, as a masterpiece of anybody's life, holds the optimal strength and growth, and which in his life is the most important thing.

The crucial question is: What is important? Today in our culture the answer to this question is different in comparison with the Middle Ages. It is still somewhat different from, let us say, the eighteenth century, at least among the people themselves. There was an idea that life is really the whole purpose of living, the purpose of being born is to make something out of this life. While today this is not important anymore. What people consider important is to be successful, to acquire power, to acquire prestige, to rise on the social ladder, to serve the machine. But they as people become stagnated; in fact, most of the people deteriorate slightly. Although they get better in the art of making money and the art of manipulating people they don't get better as human beings.

People learn nothing and have succeeded in nothing unless they think this is the most important thing to do. Those who want to learn—like most people feel today—because "It would be nice if..." will never learn anything difficult. If you want to become an expert piano player then you have to practice a few hours a day, and if you want to become a good dancer you have to do the same, and if you want to become a good carpenter you have to do the same. You do it because this is the thing you choose as the most important thing. The Talmud gives a good illustration for this: When the Hebrews were crossing the Red Sea, God, according to the Bible, told Moses to raise his staff and then the waters opened. But the Talmud says that when Moses raised his staff the waters didn't open. Only when the first Hebrew had jumped into the waters did they open, at that very moment they opened. The point is that nothing works unless someone jumps at the same time, is willing to jump. With a detached view one understands absolutely nothing of anything in this field. Because everything is swell, it doesn't get structured, it doesn't make sense, it doesn't have its right weight. One remembers it later as "well, it was a nice thing which I learned, a little this and a little that," but anything which doesn't really have an impact on one's life is really in my opinion absolutely not worthwhile learning. It's much better to go fishing, or sailing, or dancing, or anything else than to learn things which have no impact on one's life, either directly or indirectly.

What I'm saying is: If you are an apple tree, you become a good apple tree; if you are a strawberry, you become a good strawberry. I'm not speaking whether you should be a strawberry or an apple tree, because the diversity of man is tremendously great. Each person has in many ways his own entity and you might even say it's most specific, there are no persons repeated. He is unique in this sense, there is no other person exactly like him. The problem is not to create a norm for people to be the same but to create a norm that the full flowering, the full birth, the full aliveness should be in each person regardless what particular "flower" he is. That may seem to lead to a nihilistic point of view, namely that you might say: "Well, so if you are born as a criminal then you are a criminal." Frankly speaking I think it is better to be a good criminal than to be nothing. But to be nothing, to be neither criminal nor a noncriminal, to live without any purpose and consciousness—that is worse. I do think that to be a criminal, even a good criminal is indeed still a pathological phenomenon. Because man is not born to be a criminal, because criminality in itself is a pathological phenomenon.

The beginning of growth lies in the fact of becoming free. The process of freedom begins with oneself and one's parents. There is no question about it. If a person does not emancipate himself from his parents, if he or she does not feel more and more that he or she has a right to decide for himself or herself and that he or she is neither afraid nor particularly defiant toward the wishes of his or her parents, but he or she is on his or her own, then the door or the road to independence is always closed.

I would say one of the best things anybody can do is ask himself or herself: "Where am I on the personal road to independence in reference to my reaction to my parents?" I am not speaking that one shouldn't love one's parents. There is a kind of love which one can even have toward people who have damaged one, provided they did it without knowing what they were doing. Some one really couldn't blame; some are quite likeable in spite of the fact that they make many mistakes or do things wrong. So this does not refer to antagonism; those various fights against parents are usually only a smoke screen for a still existing dependence: one has to prove to the parents that they are wrong. As long as they have to prove to the parents that they are wrong, I still have to prove it to them. The question is one is free if one has neither to prove they are wrong nor that they are right. So this is me, and you are you, and if we like each other that's fine. That is the beginning of any road to freedom for oneself—of course also only to be recognized if one tries.

The Ability to Experience Reality by Oneself

Man has two faculties to judge reality. (1) He has one faculty to judge reality as it has to be judged in order to manage it. That is to say, my need to survive makes it necessary that I judge reality as I must judge it in order to manage it. If I have wood in my hands, I have to see it as wood with the specific qualities of wood if I want to make a fire. If I see somebody rushing with a weapon against me, whom I see has hostile intentions, if I believe he is the messenger of peace and has a dove in his hand, I'll be dead. That is to say, the understanding, the knowledge of reality as it is necessary to manage it, is a biologically conditioned function of man. Most people have that, and that's why they function socially.

(2) But man has another faculty. He has the function of experiencing reality not in terms of what he can do with it, but as a pure subjective experience. He looks, let us say, at a tree. Now the man who owns the tree may look at it from the standpoint: "What is it worth? Should I cut it?" He looks at the tree as a tree in terms of its sale value essentially. But if I look at the world with a subjective point of view, that is to say as something I see because I have eyes to see it, to feel, to sense, I have a sense of beauty, then I experience this tree as something wonderful—just as I can experience another person or look at a person or talk to a person. If I manipulate the person, then my question is: "What can I do with this person? What are his weak points? His strong points?" and so on. Then one's whole picture of this person is determined by the purpose of doing something with him. But if I talk to the person, like the person, don't like the person, am indifferent, look at him or her, then I have no such purposes. Then I have either a great pleasure, hopefully, or I might have a feeling of disgust, or I may have any other feelings. I may see this person—if I have the capacity to see his deepest roots, I may see this person in his whole essence, as he is.

This subjective faculty, this faculty of seeing things subjectively is the second human faculty which you find expressed for instance in poetry. If a poet writes "The rose burns like a flame," then from a standpoint of daily conventional thinking he is crazy. Take a rose and try to make a fire to boil your eggs. Obviously he doesn't refer to that; he refers to that impression which he has of this rose. He senses, he sees, he experiences the fiery burning quality of this rose. Somebody does that because he is a poet; we don't call him crazy, we call him a poet because he has at the same time the faculty to see the rose subjectively in this way, and also the faculty to see it objectively. He is clear about the fact that with this burning rose he cannot make a fire.

Most people today have lost that faculty, they can only see things as one says realistically, in the first sense, that is to say they know the world very well as it can be manipulated. But they are not capable of seeing something whether that's something in nature or a person, fully subjectively, without any other purpose except the experience of this sight, this sound, this picture. One might say then, a person is as sick when he doesn't have the faculty to see subjectively as when he fails to see outside reality. But we only call somebody psychotic and sick if he doesn't have the faculty to judge reality outside.

If a person doesn't have the faculty to see any thing subjectively we do not call him sick, or he is just as sick as the first type would be. The reason is simple: we call sick only that which interferes with social functioning. The concept of sickness is essentially social. If somebody is an idiot, is an emotional idiot, an artistic idiot, he doesn't understand a thing, he is not capable of seeing anything except the practical value of cents, then we call him today a very clever man. And these are the men who are most successful, because they are never distracted as Charlie Chaplin is in the film by the pretty girl who comes while he is working on the machines, and so he loses his grip on the machine, on the endless belt. If you feel nothing, if you have no subjective experience, then you are best fit for society in which everything that matters is to perform, to perform practically. But you are for that reason not any healthier.

The question is open who is more sick, the so-called psychotic person or the so-called realistic person. I think one can say many schizophrenics have been happier being schizophrenic than they would be working in an office trying to sell some useless commodity, or going around trying to sell it. To give a good example of this, I know of a man who was a very successful man but he was completely dominated by his wife, one of these—you all know the type: a typical Anglo-Saxon type, a tiny little woman, very modest, very thin, could hardly talk with a loud word, very very inconspicuous. She ruled the family like a dictator, but covered up by this innocent, kind of innocuous, sometimes sweet, sometimes not so sweet, but actually this kind of over-modest, over-retiring behavior. The man developed in later life a depression which forced him to be hospitalized. The doctors, very intelligently, forbade his wife to visit him, but they let his son visit him. He told his son: "You know, for the first time in my life I am happy." That sounds rather paradoxical for a depressed man at the hospital and yet it's perfectly true. For the first time in his life he felt like a free man—depression or no depression. That was the best of circumstances he could have in order to be free. Once he would be back and well—bang—he would be again the prisoner and he couldn't stand it any longer.

The Molding Impact of Society and Culture

Freud's concept was that the origin or the genesis of this particular kind of orientation—whether it is oral-receptive, oral-sadistic, or anal—lies in the fact that the libido became fixated on one of the erogenous zones. In other words here is the libido fixed at some erogenous zone by the particular fate of his libido in the course of development, and the character trait is either a sublimation or a reaction formation against this libidinal desire [...].

I believe that actually this is a secondary moment, that it isn't a fixation on some erogenous zones which is primary. But that indeed in the process of assimilating the world man has only a few possibilities: either I can get things by receiving them passively, or I can get things by taking them by force, or I can get things by hoarding them. I think there is another possibility which I mentioned in my book *Man for Himself* [1947a]: that I can get things by exchanging—and I can get things by producing them. There are no other possibilities. It depends primarily on the nature of the society, of the culture, and secondarily upon the character of the parents—not to speak of constitution of the child—which of these forms or which of these modes of assimilation will be primary in the person. And only secondarily whatever is true about the erogenous zones might appear, but really as a consequence rather than as a cause.

I do arrive to my concept of character as in fact to all other constructs, not from the development of the libido but from the character of the parents and from what I called the social character. By social character I mean that type of character which every society produces, because it needs men and makes men want to do what they have to do. To give a simple example: In the 19th century you needed people who wanted to save, because with the need of capital accumulation in that period you needed people who save, who wanted to save. So by education, by the example of the parents, by the whole upbringing of children, that type of social character which we would call an anal-hoarding character was produced. Today you need people who want to spend. So you produce the receptive and the marketing orientation, you need people who are willing to sell themselves, to be on the market. If you take a simple expression of our time, if somebody says, "I don't believe what you say," many people say "I won't buy it." That is to say that they are quite aware, although not consciously, that all—even the exchange of ideas—is a matter of the market: you buy or you don't buy.

The character orientations Freud and I have described are parallel in terms of syndromes. They are not parallel in terms of their genetic explanations. I have not made it clear enough in my writings where I see the parallel and where I don't see it. And in fact maybe I couldn't have made it clear then, because it came clear to me in the last few years really.

When one says that my ideas emphasize culture, I always feel this does not do justice to Freud, because Freud emphasizes culture, too. But there is one great difference. For Freud culture was a quantitative thing, more or less civilization, that is to say, more or less pressure or intensity of repression of instinct. While I look at culture not as a quantitative thing of more or less repression, but as a qualitative thing, namely as the different structure of any given society which forms man, which molds man, which constitutes the practice of man. In other words I assume we are what we have to be in accordance with the necessities of the society in which we live and therefore for me it's terribly important to analyze the particular structure of any given society, whether it is feudalism or nineteenth century capitalism or twentieth century capitalism or the Greek slave society. This is in the character, which is formed there for me—the essential genetic principle according to which these character-types are formed—and not the libido, the development which is dependent on certain events or certain happenings in relationship to the erogenous zones.

I am emphasizing the analysis of a particular structure of any given society, and that is what Freud did not do. This is no criticism, for he was not trained in this, but this is also what Horney and Sullivan did not do essentially, because they were not interested in an analysis of society. They were interested simply in the cultural influence—well, that's not quite fair. Horney mentions certain things which are typical for modern society, but still from my standpoint, what is necessary is to combine psychoanalysis with a strict and scientific analysis of social structure.

[The dependence of strivings from the molding social and cultural circumstances can be illustrated by sexual behavior.] Modern man consumes everything immediately, so he also consumes sex. That is part of the trend. You have nothing else in life so—and society is not endangered by that at all. On the contrary, all critical ideas, all protests against these relatively inhuman ways of living are weakened by this great venting of sex.

I'm not talking about extra-marital sexual relationships, but I talk about sexual relationships which are a kind of "instant sex," which are not accompanied by any deeper feelings or any greater depth of relationship or by any kind of *human* intimacy. I'm also not saying there's anything *wrong* with sex, because sex is an expression of life and not of death. And so I'm not saying there is something wrong with it because it is sex—in fact I think it is much better than the repressed and insincere negation of sex which was the case in the nineteenth century. But nevertheless I'm speaking from a development, from a somewhat wider standpoint, namely about the unserious, purely accidental, unintimate type of sex which is typical for today and was the privilege of the upper classes in the nineteenth century.

Many people think this kind of sex life which the new generation has created is a very new phenomenon. They forgot entirely about the upper class in England that, for instance, had this kind of life for a long time. If you read descriptions of a party in England of the upper class, the main problem of the hostess was—these people had castles of 60, 100 rooms—to put the rooms so that there was no embarrassment between the various married couples to meet each others' wives so that they didn't have to walk too long to the other bedroom. If you read the book *Jennie*, about Churchill's mother, you will find that this mother used to sleep with men who could be of use to Churchill. Churchill didn't say it in so many words, but he found that the duty of a mother was to be really helping her son in his career. There were no questions or doubts about the legitimacy, of any moral kind. So this is nothing new, this is actually one of the cases in which we can see today that the customs of the former upper classes have gone down to the middle and lower classes and that it is a cultural pattern you can see in our whole society.

The Dynamics of Psychic Development and Man's Freedom

Oswald Spengler said in his book *Untergang des Abendlandes* that the West will fall, Occidental culture will be destroyed almost as a law of nature, because his whole interpretation was that cultures grow and decay and die as a plant, as any organic being grows and dies. Rosa Luxemburg formulated her ominous view in terms of an alternative: there is a choice, there is an alternative; it can be this or that, but there is no third choice.

The difference between Spengler's and Luxemburg's view on history one should not look at only as a footnote. There are two kinds of determination. One is the one-outcome prediction: the determinism is in the sense of there is only one outcome, this will happen. Or there is the determinism of alternatives, which does not say one outcome is necessary, but a certain alternative is necessary: it can be only this or that outcome, or possibly a third one, but no other. That is particularly important with regard to the problem of determinism, not only of history or societies but with regard to men.

In regard to a person you can very rarely say—at least on sound theoretical grounds—this result is bound to happen. But you can usually say: this alternative is bound to happen. He will either grow further, to put it in very general terms, or he will die off, psychically speaking. In each case the difference being of what is the relative strength of both alternatives. The alternative that a person will humanly succeed may be one percent, but it is still an alternative and no determinism in the older sense that one is necessary.

Most people refuse to recognize in their own lives that they are really confronted with an alternative. They can go this way or that way. They think they have all sorts of choices and this is unrealistic usually, because according to their past, according to their constitution, according to their situation, we do not have any numerous choices.

[The dynamics of man's psychic development are comparable with the dynamics of playing chess:] When two players start their chances are practically even: that is to say, each one is free to win. You might say the one who has white has a slightly better chance because he starts, but we can forget about that here. Assuming they have played five moves, and white has made a mistake, then his chance to win is already reduced by sixteen percent. However, he can still win provided he makes particularly good moves afterwards, or his opponent makes a mistake. After ten more moves, white may not have compensated for his first mistake, but he may have made another mistake. Theoretically he can still win; however, his winning chance is now reduced from fifty to five percent; nevertheless he can still win. But then comes a moment when he makes another mistake. Now he cannot win at all anymore. It is impossible according to the laws of chess to win except if his opponent were so stupid that he makes a terrible blunder, which of course we cannot assume and which among good chess players doesn't happen. The good chess player at that point gives up, because he knows already he can not possibly win. The poor player goes on playing because he cannot foresee the next moves and still is hoping when in reality he couldn't win any more. He must fight it to the bitter end when he really sees that his King is checkmated and that he cannot move anymore. Then he admits that he is beaten.

What does this comparison mean applied to the human situation, to the life of all of us? Take for instance a little boy of a very well-to-do family in New York. At the age of five he was playing with a little black boy whom he liked. It was quite natural, he didn't know yet these differences. Then his mother says, in the sweet way in which modern mothers say: "You know, Johnny, I know that this boy is as good as we are, he is a fine boy, but you know the neighbors don't understand that, and really it would be better if you didn't play with him. You know I know you don't like that but I will take you to the circus tonight." Maybe she makes it even less obvious, she just doesn't say this is a reward, but she does take him to the circus or to something else or she buys him something.

Little Johnny has protested at first and has said: "No, but I like this boy!" Then he eventually accepts the invitation to the circus. That's his first mistake, his first defeat. Something has been broken in his own integrity, in his own will. He has already made, if one compares with chess, the first wrong move.

Let us say ten years later Johnny falls in love with a girl. He is really in love with her but the girl is poor, and doesn't come from the right family and the parents don't think she is a girl with whom the boy should be involved. Again in the modern fashion they don't say what their grandparents would say: "Look here, that's out of the question, that girl comes from a family with which we do not intermarry." But mother says: "This is a charming girl but you know you have different backgrounds and people must have similar backgrounds in order to make them happy. . . . But you know, you are perfectly free to marry her or not, it's entirely up to you. But you know, you can go for a year to Paris and there you can really think it over, and if you come back from Paris and still want to marry her, you marry her."

Johnny accepts it. This is the second defeat, which however is already more eased by the first defeat and by many little defeats of the same kind. He has already been bought. His self-esteem, his pride, his dignity, his sense of himself has already been broken. And since the offer is offered with this rationalization, which is so tempting because it is clothed in a form that "you are perfectly free to marry her and go to Paris," but at the moment when he accepts the ticket, he has given up the girl without knowing it. He is convinced that he still loves her and will marry her. And so the first three months he writes her the most marvellous love-letters from Paris, but his unconscious knows already that he will not marry her because he has accepted the bribe.

Once you have accepted the bribe you must deliver. Then a second moral element enters into it: you must be honest, you cannot accept a bribe without delivery, or you are dead. So in Paris, of course, he finds other girls, and so after the year many things have happened. He comes to the conclusion that now really he doesn't love that girl so much, he's fallen in love with many other girls. With a little guilty conscience, he explains to the girl why he is not in love with her. He has it easy because he just writes less and less. So the transition is not so sudden and shocking. Maybe in the meantime she got wise to the whole thing and writes him that she is through, if she has any sense.

At twenty-three Johnny is to enter graduate school. The question is what does he really want to do. His father is a very successful lawyer and his father wants him to become a lawyer, for many obvious reasons. The son, however, is really interested in architecture, was interested in that since he was a child. So he insists he wants to do the architecture. Then his father paints him a picture that he has heart trouble so that he might die soon and who will take care of the mother. After all he has done for him—the trip to Paris and so on—how ungrateful it is for the son now to desert him, and how all his hopes were, and how unhappy he would be, and besides that, what does he earn as an architect, and what does he earn in the office of his father when he becomes the chief of his office. . . . And the son puts up a little rear-guard fight and eventually he gives in. Maybe his father at this point buys him a very nice sports car. Although there are strings attached, it's never said that this is a bribe. (But that's not done in politics either: The bribe is not said with a written statement: "I give you a hundred thousand dollars so that you vote for this law." The hundred thousand dollars are given and it is understood that the other one will understand what they are given for.) At that point the young man is lost. He has completely sold himself, he has lost all his self-respect, he has lost his pride, he has lost his integrity, he does something which he doesn't like and he will then spend the rest of his life doing—probably then marrying a woman he doesn't really love, being bored with his job, and so on.

How did he get into this situation? Not by one sudden event but by the accumulation of small events, of making one mistake after the other. When he had at the beginning still much freedom, he loses this freedom more and more, up to the point where it has practically disappeared.

Freedom is not something we have; there is no such thing as freedom. Freedom is a quality of our personality: we are more or less free to resist pressure, more or less free to do what we want and to be ourselves. Freedom is always a question of increasing the freedom one has, or decreasing it. At a certain point, you might say, this young man has practically given up all hopes, although even at that point one could say an event might happen, an extraordinary event, which rarely happens in a person, on which one should not really stake one's life, but even at the age of thirty, forty, or fifty might produce a complete change and a conversion. But whoever waits for that usually waits in vain, because it is extremely rare.

· 6 ·

Factors Leading to Therapeutic Effect

On what rests the therapeutic effect of psychoanalysis? From my own point of view I would say, briefly, it rests on three factors: (1) The increase of freedom when a person can see his or her real conflicts. [(2) The increase of psychic energy after freeing it from being bound in repression and resistance. (3) Freeing the innate strivings for health.]

(1) The therapeutic effect of psychoanalysis is first based on the increase of freedom which a person has when he can see his real conflicts instead of fictional conflicts.

The real conflict of a woman (like the one reported later) can for example be her inability to emancipate herself and to start her own life, and thus her inability to be free. Her fictional conflict is: Should she marry or should she divorce her husband? That is not the real conflict. It's no conflict because it is insoluble. Her life will be miserable whether she divorces him or whether she stays with him; it will be the same miserable life as long as she is not free. But as long as she concentrates on this particular problem she cannot begin to make more sense of her life. She cannot work on her real conflict, which is that of her own freedom, of her whole relationship with the world, of her lack of interest in the world, of the great narrowness of her whole existence in the world—of all that is inaccessible to her.

To put it in a simple analogy: If you want to open the door with the wrong key, then you will never open the door. If you think you didn't put the key in right, or this or that, as long as you believe you have the right key and only think the key doesn't fit right, you'll never open the door. You have to have the right key. That's a poor analogy really. Everybody knows examples of this, where the question is: Should I do this or that and where this question is only an alleged conflict when the conflict is somewhere else entirely. Examples are to be found in one's own life or in the lives of other people, especially of elder people. One's parents are always good examples, because they have lived longer and have given you a very intimate insight into their lives if you want to look. Then you see to what extent people work on the wrong problem, try to solve something where the answer can never be found.

The following example may be an illustration of that: People marry and after three years there's a conflict so they get a divorce. What happens then? Let us say the man a year later marries exactly the same type of woman and it ends in divorce and they only stop divorcing each other when they get tired and too old, provided they have the money for all these shenanigans for such a long time. These people always think what is wrong is they didn't find the right partner. But they don't think what's wrong with themselves: what's wrong is their own incapacity to live with another person, or their own incapacity to see another person objectively and that therefore they are necessarily choosing the wrong partner. Let us say that their own narcissism makes them choose, fall in love with a woman who admires them terribly, who—let us say—tends to be submissive, and at the same time let us assume tends to be underneath quite masochistic and in the long run boring. This is indeed a bad mixture; for him, he falls in love with her because of her admiration, and after a year he sees that her submissiveness begins to bore him. At first he was happy about her submissiveness because for him her submissiveness was a great boost for his narcissism. But once he knew that she admired him so, then submissiveness like always is pretty boring, so he needs a new object to admire him and the whole circle goes on. The only solution would be if he would become aware of his narcissism or the reasons why he chooses the submissive admiring woman, and that could stop the circle.

When such a man goes to the psychoanalyst and talks about his marriage problem and how he could solve that, the only answer would be: "You have no marriage problem, you have a problem of yourself. You are the problem and you will make the same mistake as long as you do not know why you make it. If you change this, then that could be something else." To solve problems where the problems cannot be solved is a work of Sisyphus. It makes one discouraged and it takes a lot of energy because you try and try and try and by the nature of the problem you can never succeed. You sense when you try that you can never succeed. Because your whole approach is inapplicable.

Theoretically the problem is very simple, but not so easy to follow with one's own feelings what it means to try and to try and never succeed. It is as if you gather mathematical problems or other scientific problems and you start with a wrong premise. As long as you start with the wrong premise, the problem is insoluble and you get absolutely frantic and depressed. As long as you don't know that you are trying to find a solution in a way in which it cannot be found, you become more and more convinced of your powerlessness, of your own impotence, of the futility of your action, of the futility of endeavor and you become deeply discouraged. But when you see: "Oh Lord, this is not the problem, my premises are wrong; here is a real problem even if it's better, but now I can deal with it." This indeed brings new life to you, because then you think: "I may never succeed but at least this is something to work on. This is not in principle insoluble, this does not condemn me to eternal impotence. I can try to do something; I work on something meaningful rather than a fictitious problem." I think that in itself brings about an increase in freedom, in energy, in confidence, which is very important: to see the real conflicts rather than the fictitious ones.

(2) The second point is that every repression requires energy to keep the repression alive. That is to say and to put it simpler: resistance requires a lot of energy. Now this energy is taken away, is uselessly spent like we spend a considerable part of our national income for armaments. This energy is wasted. Once you lift the repression, once you don't have to feed your resistance anymore, this energy becomes available to you and the result is again an increase in energy and that means an increase in freedom. If we speak in Spinoza's terms, we might even say an increase in virtue and enjoyment.

(3) The third point I want to mention is perhaps the most important one. If I remove the obstacles which exist in myself to being in touch with what really goes on, then my innate strivings for health can begin to work. I say this on the basis of my assumption and my experience, personal as well as with others, in a very wide sense, that in every human being exists not only biologically and physiologically but also psychologically a trend toward well-being. There is nothing mysterious about that. This is, from a Darwinian standpoint very logical because well-being actually serves survival. Mental well-being serves survival in a biological sense. The more people are joyous and feel better, the longer they live, the more children they will have, the more productive they will be; but from the standpoint of biological survival, what matters is their life and that they marry and have children. That's in a very narrow sense, but I'm not speaking in this narrow sense. I quote in my book, *The Anatomy of Human Destructiveness* (1973a, pp. 254–259), a number of recent neurophysiologists who claim to me very convincingly that even in the structure of our brains we find certain propensities which are not exactly instinctive but nevertheless which are innate and

preformed, which have the tendency for well-being, for cooperation, growth.

Perhaps it will be easier to appreciate this role of the innate tendency to overcome, to grow, and to live if I remind you of emergency situations. In emergencies, people suddenly develop powers and skills which they never thought they had— not only physical powers but also mental, even powers of perception, of every kind. The reason is—and here biology really comes in—because the impulse to live is so powerfully built in the human brain that when it becomes a clear-cut matter of life or not life, an amount of energy is mobilized which was not manifest before.

For me one experience was very decisive in my thinking about that. I knew somebody in Davos who suffered from lung tuberculosis. That was at the time when you didn't have treatment by drugs, a long time ago. And she was very sick and got sicker every day. At a certain point her physician had a consultation with other specialists, and as a result he came to her and said to her: "Now, look here, we just had a consultation; there is nothing more which we can do for you from a medical standpoint. The question whether you live or die is entirely up to you." The physicians were, as one can see from this formulation, convinced that she most likely would die. Well, this did it. Within a few weeks there came a change of health which seemed to these physicians like a miracle, and this woman who was terribly sick, practically in the position of dying, got completely well. If this physician had said, as most physicians would with good intention: "Well, don't lose hope, everything will go right," he would have killed this patient, because he would have prevented her from the decisive step to mobilize her own energy.

To give another instance, I can mention Elsa Gindler in Berlin, who invented these exercises of sensing the body. How did she come to that? She suffered from tuberculosis and the doctors said to her: "If you don't go to Davos for a rest cure you will die." But she didn't have the money to go there. So she devised intuitively a system of sensing her body, that is to say, of acquiring a greater sense of bodily inner activity, of bodily equilibrium. She got completely well and developed this system which was later on taught in Germany, in Switzerland, and eventually in America. When the doctor saw her a year later on the streets, he looked up and said: "So you were in Davos," and he would hardly believe it that she wasn't.

The innate striving for health is meaningful for analytic technique as well as for one's own life without analysis. Every kind of wrong encouragement is fatal, is harmful, unless the person is so hopelessly sick that one cannot expect the full truth to have any effect any more. Otherwise, if I "encourage" a person and minimize the severity of the problem, I only damage the person, simply because I prevent emergency energy from developing. On the contrary, the more clearly and severely I describe to the person the situation he is in, and the alternatives, the more I mobilize his own emergency energies and the closer I bring him to the possibility of getting well.

· 7 ·

About the Therapeutic Relationship

The Relation Between Analyst and Analysand

It is not enough to describe the relation between analyst and analysand as an interaction. There is an interaction, but between a prison guard and a prisoner there is an interaction, too. Skinner has gone in his book *Beyond Freedom and Dignity* (1971) so far to state that the man who is tortured controls the torturer as much as the torturer controls him, because by his shouts of pain he tells the torturer what means to apply. In a perverse way, one might say in a certain sense Skinner is right, but only in a very absurd sense, because essentially the torturer controls his sacrifice and there is indeed some interaction, but it is negligible, as far as the question is concerned about who controls whom.

I don't want to compare the family situation with that of the torturer and the tortured, but I am mentioning this drastic example to question the concept of interaction. It's perfectly true, the interaction is there, but in any interaction you have to raise one question. Who is the one in this interaction who has the power to force the other one? Is it an interaction of equals or is it an interaction of unequals who basically cannot fight on the same level? The academic sociological concept of interaction implies a great danger. It is purely formalistic; that is to say, the interaction is wherever two people interact.

One has to determine whether the quality of interaction is one of equality or one of control, of greater force by the one who can force the other to act as he wishes. A classic expression for this question is to be found in international and also in civil treaties. If a very strong power makes an alliance with a very small power, it is phrased in terms of an alliance; that is to say, even the annexation is phrased in terms of a treaty of equals. But what is certain in these treaties is that *de facto* all the rights, except usually language, are to a greater power—but formally it is a treaty. The same old story in business—and the Roman law called that a *societas leonina*, a Lion Society: a big firm makes an association, a contract of fusion with small firms. Legally it reads as if the two make a free contract, but in fact the big firm simply takes over the small firm; but this is not expressed in these legal terms, it is expressed that the two are perfectly free to make a contract while the small firm is not free at all. That interaction of itself is not enough. This interaction is too formal; although it's real enough, it's too abstract. What matters in all human relationships is primarily the relatively free unjealous power of two partners.

In this respect I have a different experience from that of Freud—actually I have both experiences because I have been trained at an orthodox Freudian institute in Berlin, and practiced as an orthodox Freudian analyst for about 10 years until I became more and more dissatisfied with what I experienced. I noticed I became bored during the hour. The main difference is to be seen in the following: Freud saw the whole analytic situation as a laboratory situation; here was a patient who is an object; the analyst as a laboratory man watches what comes out of the mouth of this object. Then he draws all sorts of conclusions, gives back to the patient whatever he sees. In this respect I am also on the opposite side of Dr. Rogers. I think the whole expression "client-centered therapy" is kind of strange because every therapy has to be client-centered. If the analyst is such a narcissist that he cannot be centered on the client, he really shouldn't do the job he is doing. I don't think client-centered therapy, which is something self-evident, means just mirroring, on the contrary.

What do I do? I listen to the patient and then I say to him: "Look, what we are doing here is the following. You tell me whatever comes to your mind. That will not always be easy; sometimes you will not want to tell me. All I ask you in that case is to say that there is something you won't tell me, because I don't want to put any more pressure on you that you have to do things. Probably in your life you have been told much too often that you have to do something. Alright, but I would appreciate it if you would tell me that you are leaving out something. So I listen to you. And while I am listening I have responses which are the responses of a trained instrument, I just am trained in this. So what you tell me makes me hear certain things and I tell you what I hear, which is quite different from what you are telling me or intended to tell me. And then you tell me how you respond to my response. And in this way we communicate. I respond to you, you respond to my response, and we see where we are going." I am very active in this.

I don't interpret; I don't even use the word interpretation. I say what I hear. Let us say the patient will tell me that he is afraid of me and he will tell me a particular situation, and what I "hear" is that he is terribly envious; let us say he is a oral-sadistic, exploitative character and he would really like to take everything I have. If I have the occasion to see this from a dream, from a gesture, from free associations, then I tell him: "Now, look here, I gather from this, that, and the other that you are really afraid of me because you don't want me to know that you want to eat me up." I try to call his attention to something he is not aware of. The whole point here is that there are some analysts, Rogers most extremely so, some Freudian analysts less extremely so, who believe the patient should find it himself. But I think that prolongs the process tremendously; it is long enough and difficult enough anyway. What happened? There are certain things in the patient which he represses; and he represses it for good reasons; he doesn't want to be aware of them; he is afraid of being aware of them. If I sit there and wait for hours and months and years perhaps, until these resistances are broken through, I waste time for the patient.

I am doing the same thing that Freud does in dream interpretation. The dream may be a harmless dream, and yet what Freud says is, this dream really says you want to kill me. I do that with other things, too. I tell the patient what I see and then I analyze the patient's resistance to what I am saying. Or, if there is not much resistance, then the patient will feel it, but I am very aware of the fact that intellectualization doesn't help a bit, in fact it makes everything impossible. What matters is whether the patient can feel what I am referring to.

Spinoza has said knowledge of the truth in itself changes nothing unless it is also an affective knowledge. This holds true for all psychoanalysis. You may analyze and find out that you suffer from a depression because as a child you were neglected by your mother. You can find that out and believe that until doomsday and it'll not do you the slightest good. Maybe that's exaggerated, it may be a little help, you know the reason but it's like the exorcism of the devil. You say, "That's the devil," and if you have done that for many years by the way of suggestion, eventually if the patient feels he has exorcised the devil—and the mother who rejected him is the devil—then he may eventually feel less depressed if the depression was not so serious. To know what is repressed means really to experience it here, not only in thought but to fully feel it. This kind of experience has in itself a very relieving effect. It is not the question of explaining something: "This is because—," but of really feeling. In the kind of an x-ray you feel in depth: here I am depressed. If you really feel it, that promotes the idea to do something to clear the depression and you can come to the next stage where you maybe feel: "I am really furious and I punish my wife with my depression." On the other hand, the person may be so sick or the depression may be so severe that even that does not help.

Preconditions of the Psychoanalyst

For every psychoanalytic work there is one important aspect: the personal qualities of the analyst. The primary thing here is his experience and his understanding of another human being. Many analysts become analysts because they feel very inhibited to reach human beings, to relate to human beings, and in the role of an analyst they feel protected, especially if they sit behind the couch. But it is not only that. It is also very important that the analyst is not afraid of his own unconscious and therefore he is not afraid to open up the patient's unconscious and that he is not embarrassed about it.

This leads me to what you might call the humanistic premise of my therapeutic work: There is nothing human which is alien to us. Everything is in me. I am a little child, I am a grown up, I am a murderer, and I am a saint. I am narcissistic, and I am destructive. There is nothing in the patient which I do not have in me. And only inasmuch as I can muster within myself those experiences which the patient is telling me about, either explicitly or implicitly, only if they arouse and echo within myself can I know what the patient is talking about and can I give him back what he is really talking about. Then something very strange happens: The patient will not have the feeling I am talking *about* him or her, nor that I talk down to him or her, but the patient will feel that I am talking about something which we both share. The Old Testament says: "Love the stranger, because you have been strangers in Egypt and therefore you know the soul of the stranger."[Deut. 10:19]

One knows another person only inasmuch as one has experienced the same. To be analyzed oneself means nothing else but to be open to the totality of human experience which is good and bad, which is everything. I heard a sentence from Dr. Buber recently about Adolf Eichmann, that he could not have any particular sympathy with him although he was against the trial, because he found nothing of Eichmann in him. Now, that I find an impossible statement. I find the Eichmann in myself, I find everything in myself; I find also the saint in myself, if you please.

If I am analyzed that means really—not that I have discovered some childish traumata, this or the others primarily—it means that I have made myself open, that there is a constant openness to all the irrationality within myself, and therefore I can understand my patient. I don't have to look for them. They are there. Yet my patient analyzes me all the time. The best analysis I ever had is as an analyst and not as a patient, because inasmuch as I try to respond to the patient and to understand, to feel what goes on in this man or woman, I have to look into myself and to mobilize those very irrational things which the patient is talking about. If the patient is frightened and I repress my own fright I will never understand the patient. If the patient is a receptive character and I cannot mobilize that in me which is receptive or was receptive but is still there, at least in a small dose, I will never understand it.

The training curriculum of psychoanalysts should include the study of history, history of religion, mythology, symbolism, philosophy, that is to say all of the main products of the human mind. Instead of that, today officially the requirement is that he studies psychology and has a doctor's degree in psychology. Well, I think that is—and I am sure many psychologists agree with me—simply a waste of time. They do it only because they are forced to do it, because otherwise they do not get the degree which the state recognizes, that is a condition for their being licensed as psychotherapists. In academic psychology, which you study in universities, you hear practically nothing about men in the sense in which psychoanalysis deals with men in order to understand their motivations, to understand their problems; at best you have something like behaviorism, which by definition excludes the understanding of man, basically, because it really emphasizes all that we have to study in the behavior of man and how this behavior is manipulated.

The analyst should not be naive; that is to say, he should know the world as it is and should be critical toward what happens. How can one be critical about the psyche of another person, about his consciousness, if one is not at the same time critical about the general consciousness and the forces which are real in the world? I do not believe one can. I do not believe that truth is divisible, that one can see the truth in personal matters but be blind in all other matters. One can see the truth to some extent in personal matters, but one can never see it if one's mind is half blinded. If one's mind is completely awake and open, then indeed he can see whether it's a person or whether it's society, whether it's the situation or anything, or whether it's art.

One has to be critical and to see what is behind the appearances. I do believe that one cannot understand a person, an individual, unless one is critical and understands the forces of society which have molded this person, which have made this person what he or she is. To stop at the story of the family is just not enough. For the full understanding of the patient it is not enough either. He will also only be fully aware of who he is if he is aware of the whole social situation in which he lives, all the pressures and all the factors which have their impact on him. I do believe that psychoanalysis is essentially a method of critical thought, and to think critically is indeed very difficult because it is in conflict with one's advantages. No one is particularly promoted for thinking and being critical. Nobody has any advantage for it, except maybe in the long run.

In my opinion social analysis and personal analysis cannot really be separated. They are part of the critical view of the reality of human life. Perhaps it is much more useful to the understanding of psychoanalysis to read Balzac than it is to read psychological literature. Reading Balzac trains one better in the understanding of man in analysis than all the analytic forces in the world, because Balzac was a great artist who was able to write case histories, but with what richness, with what wealth, really going down to the unconscious motivations of people and showing them in their interrelations to the social situation. That was the attempt of Balzac: he wanted to write the character of the French middle class of his time. If one is really interested in man and in his unconscious, don't read the textbooks, read Balzac, read Dostoyevsky, read Kafka. There you learn something about man, much more than in psycho-analytic literature (including my own books). There one find a wealth of deep insight, and that is what psychoanalysis could do, should do with regard to individuals.

What people and especially analysts today ought to learn first of all is to see the distinction between authenticity and façade. Actually that sense is greatly weakened today. Most people take words for reality; that's already a crazy, insane confusion. But I think also most people do not see the difference between façade and the authentic, although unconsciously they do. You can often find a dream in which a person has seen a man in the daytime and he thought he was very nice and he liked him, and then he has a dream in which he sees this person as a murderer, or a thief, which simply meant subliminally he was aware that this man is dishonest. But in his consciousness he was not aware while he saw him. Of course, you don't assume somebody is a murderer—I don't mean realistically murderer, but in his intentions—or that somebody is destructive unless we have proven it, or maybe the man said something to him and so he was flattered. In our dreams we are usually honest, much more honest than we are in the daytime, because we are not influenced by events from the outside.

Dealing with the Patient

[To begin a therapeutic relation, mutual trust must be presupposed. If a patient asks me whether I trust him, I shall answer:] "I trust you at the moment but I have no reason to trust you and you have no reason to trust me. Let's see what happens, whether we can trust each other after a while when we have had some contact." If I'd said: "Of course I trust you!" I would be lying. How can I trust him unless he is a very exceptional person? Sometimes I trust a person after seeing him or her five minutes. Sometimes I know definitely I don't trust somebody. That's then too bad because that's no basis for analysis.

Not to start analysis depends on many things. If I have an impression that I don't trust this person, but I still see there is something in which he or she could change, I might tell him or her that I really don't find him or her very trustworthy but still I think maybe there is something. Or if that is not the case, I would find some reason without offending him or her, to say that I don't think we are very well prepared to work together, he (or she) had better go to somebody else.

I would never say to anybody in the world—and I have never said so—that he or she could not be analyzed or he or she could not be helped. I am deeply convinced that that is a statement for which nobody can be responsible. I am not God and there is no way of knowing definitely if a person is hopeless or not. My own judgment can be that he or she is, but how can I trust my own judgment to that extent that I would speak a verdict about that person and say somebody else could not help him? So I have never ended an initial interview or any initial work with this statement. If I have felt I was not in a position to work with that person, I have tried to send him or her to somebody else—and this I did not as an excuse but because I deeply believe it is my obligation to give him or her any chance he or she has, and my judgment is certainly not enough to base such a vital decision on.

As far as reducing dependency is concerned, that is a matter of dosage in every case. If you have a patient who is a near schizophrenic with an extreme—what I would call—symbiotic attachment to his or her analyst, in which the person feels absolutely lost, if he or she does not have that unshakeable or unbreakable tie with the host person, you will find in many pre-schizophrenic or schizophrenic patients that there is a symbiotic relationship to the mother or father figure. That is the moment where they should be confronted with the necessity to stand on their own feet—although there might be the danger of a psychotic breakdown. In a symbiotic relationship, I would put it this way: The process of individuation has not occurred in spite of the fact that the person is beyond adolescence.

Freud believed that by examining, by studying the depth of a person, his insight into the processes going on in his very depth should lead to a change in his personality, to a cure of symptoms. I like to call attention to the fact of how extraordinary this idea was, especially if you consider the present time, and some people said so even then, many years ago—to devote that much time to one person is not in the contemporary mood. On the contrary, since everything has to be done in a hurry, the most important objection to analysis is it still takes so much time.

Quite surely a bad analysis should be as short as possible, but a deep and effective analysis should last as long as necessary. Naturally one should try methods to make it last no longer than necessary but the idea that it is worthwhile to devote that attention for hundreds and hundreds of hours to one person is in itself, I would say, an expression of a deep humanism in Freud. The reason that a psychoanalysis takes too long in itself is not a reason against it, and if one presents it as a social problem, it is a sheer rationalization. That is to say, one really rationalizes one's ideas that a person doesn't deserve that much attention, that that person is not that important. One rationalizes that by presenting a viewpoint, a social viewpoint, that only the ones that are better off get this treatment.

The idea that the patient must pay for the treatment, otherwise he can't get well, is like the opposite of what the Gospel says, the rich will never go to Heaven. I think it's plain nonsense. Because the real question is what effort somebody makes; for a very rich person paying for the treatment means absolutely nothing. In fact, it's a deduction from taxes which is always desirable. So if a person shows no interest whether he pays or doesn't pay, that's the only criterion, and it's a very self-serving rationalization that he has to pay—the more he pays, the quicker he gets well, because he makes more of a sacrifice. It's the thinking really of modern times, that what you pay for you value most, and what you don't pay for you value little. If you pay much then you may value analysis even less because you are accustomed to buying. That's a fact. People don't value, particularly when they have money; they don't value particularly what they buy.

[In regard to group-psychotherapy] I am very suspicious, but I have to say I have never done group-therapy and probably precisely because I dislike it tremendously. I just dislike the idea of one person talking intimately about himself in front of ten other people. I couldn't stand it. I also have the suspicion that this is the psychoanalysis for the man who cannot pay twenty-five dollars, but if ten get together, you pay fifty and that's fine.

Actually I can imagine that especially for adolescents group-therapy might be very useful. If they are not very sick, have similar problems, it might help them to see that they have common problems and on a superficial basis with some good teaching, some good advice, I think their problems might be alleviated and it is a very good thing. But I do not think it is in any way a substitute for psychoanalysis. Psychoanalysis is a method which is so individualized and so personal that I don't think it lends itself to the method of group-therapy. I am in this respect an individualist and an old-fashioned man.

I believe that atmosphere which we are seeing today, reduces privacy more and more for the sake of common chatter and leads to an anti-human and anti-humanist attitude. I don't think it is conducive to any good therapy except in very specific cases where I do not want more. The statement that the relation to the patient is artificial—that doesn't impress me. A love-relationship between two people is also artificial because they don't make love in society and their most intimate hour is not shared by ten other people. I think there is a lot of rationalization in an age in which privacy gets lost more and more.

· 8 ·

Functions and Methods of the Psychoanalytic Process

Mobilizing Unconscious Energies and Showing Alternatives

The mobilization of the latent energies of a person is actually the central issue of all analytic work. For this I can give an example. I remember a man in his forties who came to me and said: "Well, what chance do I have to get well?" He had lived with some neurotic symptoms but he muddled through and he functioned. I said to him: "Frankly speaking if it was a question of betting, I would not bet that you will get well, because you have lived with your same problems for forty years and there is no reason that you should get insane or die earlier. So you will live another thirty years in the same way and will be unhappy but as you have borne it so far, why shouldn't you for the rest of your life? Apparently it's not that bad." Then I said to him: "If you have an extremely strong will and wish to really change your life, then maybe there is a possibility; I'm willing on this chance to analyze you, but if you ask me what I think objectively what are the chances, the chances are that it's not very probable that you will succeed."—If there's anything which can encourage a patient it is that. But if he is discouraged, then he might better not begin, because if he cannot take this then he will lack in that basic impulse, namely, to have the strength to mobilize his energy.

What I just said does not hold true in all cases. There are people for instance who are so frightened, hypochondriacal and panicky and anxious that if you tell them they get into a panic that prevents them from thinking. In such cases you have to react in a different way. I am speaking about this in a general sense to make clear the importance it has, not only in analysis but in every life, to see their intelligence clearly. If one would ask why most people fail in life, I think the reason is that they never know when the decisive moment comes. If I knew right now if I do this—let us say: to accept a bribe directly or indirectly—I will end as a broken man because I will go on accepting bribes, I will submit, and I will eventually land as an unhappy broken man. If I knew this then this sense of being well and the emergency energies would work enough in many people to make them decide with "no." But prefer to rationalize: "Well, this is only one step, it's not so important, I might do this eventually, I can still change." So there is never a moment in the life of many people when they are aware, when they are in the situation of being able—this is a decision and they become aware of it when it is much too late. Then indeed, retrospectively, one can say their life was determined and they had never a chance for freedom. But you can only say that restrospectively. If they had seen the situation and confronted the fact that when they go here this will lead to this result, then indeed they would have had a chance to act entirely differently because they were not that sick then and had not broken then.

To speak of analysis I consider it a very important task of the analyst to show the person whom he analyzes the real alternatives, very drastically and not pussyfooting, and maybe to put it in careful terms so that one says and doesn't say it. If the person who is analyzed has a resistance and doesn't want to see clearly, the use of words which are not quite clear leads to the fact that he hears nothing because he doesn't want to hear anything. You must shout, now sometimes literally, but I don't mean it literally; shout in the sense of a statement which he cannot bypass, to which he has to react because it is too challenging.

The main reason why this awareness of oneself, the true awareness of one's whole situation, has a chance to change is that it permits these energies which are in us to operate. And if they are not there, if they are dead already, then there is nothing one can do. One has—and analysts especially have to have—a great deal of faith in the existence of these energies without being foolish. There are many people in whom they are so weak that there is nothing more to be done—it may be a matter of age, it may be a matter of having already been so beaten down that you see there is no more hope. It would be foolish to say, as a matter of dogma or principle, this person will react positively to the full confrontation with his life. He may not, but on the whole it may help him to be aware of where he is going, of the alternatives in his whole existence. This is one of the most important tasks which the analyst has.

To help the analysand to get aware of his alternatives is part of analyzing him. It is not expressing value judgments; this is just stating—in fact I can state them in any other field—these are the forces and if you go this way this will happen; if you go that way that will happen. These are the alternatives which by themselves determine there is no other way. Most people think and feel for this fact that there is always the impossible solution. You want to be free but you want to remain in the stable with your parents. You want to be free and you want to be dependent. This doesn't work; you can't, it's a mere fiction. Just as you cannot have people who are independent and free and at the same time have stultified them by mass advertising and by the kind of things people learn. You can't have both; but most people want to compromise and this is, you might say, one of the forms of resistance. As long as I hope for the miracle, which means an impossible solution, which is realistically impossible as long as it exists, naturally I have no chance of doing anything.

Sublimation, Satisfaction, or Renunciation of Sexual Strivings

In the first place the whole concept of sublimation is a most questionable concept. I doubt very much if there is such a thing as sublimation really. But it's a very popular concept, it goes in so easily. Sublimation—you think of a chemical reaction and here you have your base drives, and then it's all sublimated.

I want to illustrate my doubts with a simple example. The general psychoanalytic concept was, a surgeon sublimates his sadisms or—in a later version—his death instinct. That is to say, he has really an urge to hurt, an urge to torture, but instead of expressing it directly he expresses it on a level which is far away from the direct, as Freud would say, libidinous expression, and at that point it is hidden. This is, I think without any doubt, not so. The surgeon has an entirely different motivation. There are, of course, surgeons who might have been motivated by their wish to hurt, but I'm sure they're the poorest surgeons in the world; they make very poor surgeons.

On the contrary a surgeon is motivated by a wish for quick action, for quick healing, by a gift of making quick decisions, by technical gift of dexterity of his hands, and so the surgeon is acting upon impulses or a foundation of very normal human gifts and desires. These are the ways in which his talents go, and that's why he is cool, and objective, and very rational in his surgical work. If the surgeon were a hidden sadist then he would be exactly lacking these qualities, he would have a kind of hidden pleasure, he would operate when he shouldn't, he would cut people when he shouldn't, he would be driven by that impulse he is sublimating: it is there. It is not suddenly out of nothing. Besides that, you must say, you might sublimate your sadism but you still remain a sadistic character. Whether surgeons have more often sadistic characters than psychoanalysts let us say remains an open question more than any other branch of medicine, or, for heaven's sake, teachers.

If one would say many teachers are sadists who wish to control, that's perfectly true, but I don't think one can say they're sublimated; they give a very direct expression to their sadism in forms which are adequate under the circumstances. Some teachers really beat up the children, violently, in systems in which they're not punished for it, and there's nothing of sublimation to it. The others just hurt their self-esteem, hurt their sensitivities, hurt their dignity, and do in words what the other one does with a stick. Where is the sublimation—nowhere? Everybody expresses his passion in those forms which are the least dangerous under the circumstances but have exactly the same function. So I would say this whole concept of sublimation is really untenable.

Many people do something which they really want to get rid of but they do it in the thought, if I experience it fully that helps me to become fully aware of it and to overcome it. But usually it has no such function. One knows what it is; it's nothing new; one doesn't experience it any deeper. I think this reasoning is basically resistance. One cannot change these things by force either.

Here again I would say analysis and practice should go together. Somebody would say, I stop it right now. I think that's one way of solving it, maybe a good one. On the other hand the other way round—to say, I follow it because the more I do it the more I will learn about myself—I think that's a rationalization. The optimum perhaps is to begin to fight with it, but to see what I do experience if I restrict it, if I renounce it quantitatively; what I do experience in the act of renunciation, rather than dogmatically make a step which breaks down after three months because one wasn't ready for it. In other words a certain change in behavior with simultaneous analysis of the experiences in changing it, I would think, is the optimum one can do. That's about the answer I can give to that but again this is such a general problem that all general answers are much lacking, because one cannot deal with them in a more specific way. So there is really no answer, basically, which is generally true for anyone specifically. In each situation and in each person the answer is somewhat different, and one can also never be sure that it's right.

That renunciation and the analysis of renunciation is more valuable than acting out and the analysis of actions has to do with the fact that it is new. What I experience in the sadistic experience that I know. Naturally one should analyze the sadistic experience to its full context and not just talk about sadism,but go into every detail: what do I feel, what does it mean, what has it to do with sadistic tendencies in general? I am assuming this is done fully, but then once this is done new factors come to light if one sees what happens if I change. What happens if I act differently? Because this brings new experience: I have never tried it in such a way that at the same time I analyzed it.

First you might find that the person in doing this tries to stop it at a certain moment because of an attack of deep anxiety and of deep insecurity. That's exceedingly helpful because then we can see that this behavior is a protection against anxiety. Then we can go and analyze the anxiety. But as long as one goes on doing it, this anxiety might not come out. In fact that holds true for all frustration of things one does; they usually have the function to prevent manifest anxiety from coming out. This anxiety does not become manifest unless you stop it.—I don't want to be misunderstood. It is not the question that one has to stop it and "schluss." But the ability to renounce it is a condition of further treatment and for salvation. I also don't mean an act of force at all. I only mean this as an experiment: to stop it for a week, for two weeks, and see what happens. That's a very different story from saying you must not ever do that again. That's a threat, that's blackmail, and that never works.

In general much anxiety which is the basis for the development of a symptom becomes visible, becomes open only when the symptom is frustrated. Freud says that, and I think he was basically right in this: "Analytic treatment should be carried through, as far as is possible, under privation—in a state of abstinence." (S. Freud, 1919a, S.E., vol. 17, p. 162.) Perhaps he went a little far with this. But basically if you act out the very thing you want to analyze, that you want to get rid of, then indeed there are very great limitations to what you can do analytically, because you do not get at the underlying anxiety. You do not get on the question of what defenses you have built with your symptom, what resistances are in this symptom, and so on.

In my opinion perversions should be treated only if the person suffers from it, that is to say, if the person feels that this is something which disturbs him very much, which splits up his life, which goes against his values, which if he can discover the relationship it has to his character, his relationship to other people. Otherwise I do not consider it something which has to be treated. But I do consider it a serious problem because one has to ask oneself what is the connection—and this is important—between the so-called perversion and the characterological elements in one. To what extent is it really a regression or a fixation or a stage where one stands in one's own way to a fuller relationship, not only to women or to people. It's in a way a similar problem as that of homosexuality. I don't think homosexuality is a sickness, but nevertheless I think it is a restriction in the growth of a person, but less so than sado-masochistic perversion. So to sit on a high horse and to say that the homosexuals have no real love and are so narcissistic and so on—what the hell, who is talking?

About the Recognition of Resistance

Perhaps the most important thing in analysis is the recognition of resistance. There's one analyst who recognized this resistance first and most thoroughly: Wilhelm Reich. That is in fact his main contribution to analysis. I think his other contributions are very doubtful or questionable. He made another contribution which is equally important—that he was, after Georg Groddek, the only one who saw the importance of loosening up the body in order to overcome repression. When he wrote his book *Character analysis* (W. Reich, 1933), he emphasized this.

Resistance is one of the trickiest things, not only in analysis, but also in the life of everybody who tries to grow, who tries to live. Man seems to have two very strong tendencies. One is to move forward, starting you might say from the beginning of the birth of a child, the impulse to be impelled to get out of the womb, but at the same time a great fear of all that is new, all that is different, you might say a fear of freedom, a fear of the risk, and an almost equally strong tendency to recoil, to go back, not to move forward. This fear of the new, this fear of that to which one is not accustomed, this fear of that which is not certain because one has never experienced it, all this fear is expressed in resistances, in various manoeuvres to prevent one from moving forward, from doing something daring.

Resistance is by no means a problem of analysis only. Most problems in fact which are discussed in analysis, like resistance or transference, are much more important as general human problems. As analytic problems they are relatively restricted, so how many people are analyzed? But in general human terms resistance and transference are among the most powerful emotional forces which exist.

We are never trickier than when we are rationalizing our resistances. Not the least of all resistance is to get better; any improvement is to be looked at with great suspicion, rather than with satisfaction and joy. Because very often the improvement serves only to begin the compromise, to have satisfied oneself: "You see I'm not as sick as I was," but at the same time now it's enough, to prevent one from the decisive step which could radically solve the problem by going forward. So it is very important to be skeptical towards improvements. Defeats are better than successes, provided as Nietzsche said: "What doesn't kill us makes us stronger" ("Was uns nicht umbringt, macht uns stärker") (F. Nietzsche, 1889, nr. 8). There are certain defeats which are fatal, but on the whole success is the one most dangerous thing in which people fail. And it usually serves as a resistance to go further.

Now resistance has, of course, many other forms; one person expresses resistance by flooding the analyst with dreams, so from then on one listens to dreams for years; they are the good dreamers and nothing is ever analyzed because the dream is very alienated; one analyzes the dream but one doesn't analyze the person.

Another form of resistance is trivial talk. Freud's great idea was to put free association as a substitute for hypnosis. So he thought if he touched the forehead of a person and said: "Whenever I touch your forehead then you say whatever comes to mind," that was a more successful shorter kind of hypnotic suggestion. There is much truth in that, but in the meantime that was given up and the formula said: "You say everything that comes to your mind." So the person talks about all the trivialities of life, repeats a hundred thousand times what his mother said, his father said, what the husband said, what a quarrel they had, and the analyst listens dutifully because the patient talks about what goes through his mind. That, of course, is a form of resistance which an analyst should never permit, because it's utterly irrelevant to listen to all the banal details of this or that quarrel and to repetitions of all these personal things which are useless—are just filling out the time. They are essentially resistance.

I remember a seminar at the William Alanson White Institute where an analyst had presented a patient, and I listened for an hour and then I said: "Look here, this is so trivial I can't see how you can stand listening to that for an hour. It's all about the calls which she had with her boyfriend, back and forth and then psychologizing, should she have called him up or should she not have called him up, as if that were any matter of significance." He said: "Well, but no, she was very serious, it was a real problem to her." And then he was very generous and said "All right, I have a tape." He asked the patient for permission to play the tape, and once it had started after five minutes the whole class laughed and he too because it was perfectly obvious from her voice she was as unserious as anybody could be. It was nothing, it had no meaning, no sense. In other words, free association has been transformed into free chatter. And "free chatter" is absolutely dead as soon as a person begins to chatter and to speak about things which have no meaning except that they are considered a psychological problem. Everything is a psychological problem. Then it is in my opinion the task of the analyst to cut him off and to say: "Now, all you're telling me is only to fill out the time, and it has no purpose; I'm too bored, I'm not going to listen to this." Why should I? It's indecent to listen to boring stuff for an hour and you can't be paid for that. No sum is big enough to pay for this sacrifice; in fact it would be indecent to accept the money for this kind of stuff.

In many instances you have a kind of gentleman's agreement that both are very secret, that both the patient and the analyst agree they won't deprive each other of his or her sleep. The patient wants the satisfaction to talk and to be analyzed and to improve, and to find herself or himself, and the analyst must make a living anyway, he doesn't want to be too disturbed either, everything should go smoothly, and so after a while they find a status or a level in which really one talks about so-called significant problems, and yet nobody is really disturbed. Now

I'm not saying that is the case with all analyses. Freudian or not Freudian—it doesn't make the slightest difference, it's just a difference in idiom whether you talk a hundred times about fixation to your father and you are interested in this boy because he is a father-figure, or whether you talk about your not getting enough love from your mother and that's why you fall in love with this girl who gives you much love, and all that stuff. It remains meaningless and it's one of the main reasons for resistance.

Transference, Counter-transference, and the Real Relation

Another important problem relevant for the therapeutic process is transference. Transference is about the most significant problem in human life. [Cf. also E. Fromm, 1990a, pp. 45–52.] If one asks why people have sacrificed their children for the Moloch, why people have worshipped idols like Mussolini or Hitler, why people have given their lives for some ideological idol, it's all the same phenomenon of transference. The whole Freudian analytic concept of transference is much too narrow. What Freud meant by this, and most analysts still do mean by it, is what the word says: you transfer an affect which once referred to the significant people in your childhood—your father and mother—to the analyst. That is to a large extent too true.

Harry Stack Sullivan used as an example for transference a person whom he analyzed for a week; after a week this person remarked while saying goodbye: "But doctor, you don't have a beard." Sullivan had a little moustache but was otherwise clean shaven. For a week she had believed he had a beard, because indeed he was so much the father for her that the whole image if her father who had a beard was literally transferred to him. She saw in him the father even visually, optically, because her feelings were that he was her father, they were of the same nature. This is a narrower concept of transference: the transferred feelings of the child to a significant person, to another person. But this is not perhaps the essence of transference. Much more important is transference in a very general sense.

Transference expresses a need of a person to have somebody who takes over the responsibility, who is a mother, who gives unconditional love, who is a father who praises and punishes, and admonishes and teaches. And even if people had never had a father and a mother, even if people had never been children, they need that as long as they have not become fully human themselves, fully independent themselves. If you want to understand the need for such people whom one considers as the guides, as the protectors, as the gods and goddesses, it is not enough to think of childhood. You have to consider the whole human situation in which man is so helpless, so confused to a large extent by the misinformation he gets about life through his culture, so frightened, so uncertain that it is a general human longing to have somebody whom you can choose as your idol, to whom you can say: "This is my god." This is the person who loves me, who guides me, who rewards me, because I cannot stand of myself.

Transference is a result of the failure in one's own freedom and thereby is the result of the need to find an idol to worship, to believe in in order to overcome one's fear and uncertainty about the world. The adult human being is in a way not less helpless than the child. He *could* be less helpless if he or she grows up to be a fully independent, developed human being, but if he or she doesn't, then indeed he or she is just as helpless as a child, because he or she sees himself or herself surrounded by a world over which he or she has no influence, which he doesn't understand, which leaves him in uncertainty and fear and therefore while a child seeks an adult—the father or mother—for, let us say, biological reasons, the grown-up person seeks the same for social and historical reasons.

Transference is a phenomenon which you find in the relatedness of—let us say—a neurotic person or an unrealistic person as much as to a psychoanalyst, also to many other people: to a teacher, to a wife, to a friend, to a public figure. I would define transference in psychoanalysis as the irrational relatedness to another person which can be analyzed in the analytical procedure, while transference in other situations is one which is just the same, depending on the rationality of the person, but it is not open to analysis, it is not on the table of operation.

If somebody is impressed by power, somebody wants to be protected by a powerful person, you will have the same worship and the same overestimation of his analyst as he has of his professor, or of a governmental figure, or he has of his minister or priest or what's not what. It's always the same mechanism. Only in analysis this particular kind of irrational relatedness, which corresponds to a need of him, is brought to analysis.

Transference is not a simple repetition; but what we are dealing with is the need of a person to have another person to fulfill this need. For instance, if I feel weak, uncertain, afraid of risks, afraid of decisions—I may want to find a person who is certain, who is prompt, who is powerful, in whom I can take refuge. Naturally I seek that all my life. This will be the kind of boss I seek for, or a professor if I am student—and this is what I shall see in the analyst. On the other hand, I am a very narcissistic person who thinks everybody else is an idiot; provided he criticizes me I will think that the analyst is an idiot, my teacher is an idiot, my boss is an idiot, everybody else is. These are all the same phenomenon of transference, except in analysis we call it transference when we can analyze it.

Analyst and analysand meet really on two separate levels, one is that of transference, and the other is that of counter-transference. In regard to counter-transference it holds true: the analyst has all sorts of irrational attitudes toward the patient. He is afraid of the patient, he wants to be praised by the patient, he wants to be loved by the patient. It's too bad, it shouldn't be that way, he should by his own analysis have achieved a position where he doesn't need all that love, but this is really not always the case.

I think it is a mistake to believe that all that goes on between the analyst and the patient is transference. This is only one aspect of the relationship; but the more fundamental aspect is: there is a reality of two people talking together, which in the day of the telephone and radio is not taken as a very serious reality, but to me it is one of the most serious realities. One person talks to another. They don't talk about trivial things; they talk about something very important namely the life of this person.

Quite aside from transference and counter-transference, the therapeutic relationship is characterized by the fact that there are two real persons involved, and the patient who is not psychotic has a sense of what the other person is and the analyst has a sense of what the patient is, and that is not all transference. I think one very important fact of psychoanalytic technique is that the analyst must constantly, so to speak, scrabble on two tracks: he must offer himself as an object of transference and analysis, but he must offer himself also as a real person and respond as a real person.

Remarks on Working with Dreams

Dream interpretation is about the most important instrument we have in psychoanalytic therapy. There is nothing the patient can say, associations, slips of the tongue, and whatever it may be, which is as significantly revealing as dreams, and I believe as Freud says that dreaming and dream interpretation really is the "royal road" of understanding the unconscious. On the question of my view on the difference between Freud and Jung, I am indeed neither of the one nor the other opinion.

Freud not only pointed out that the dream refers to the past, that is to say rarely desires, instinctual desires, which come up in the dream and which are rooted in the past, but Freud assumed also that really the dream text is necessarily distorted and that the real meaning of the dream, namely what Freud called the latent dream, has to be snatched from the manifest dream text. On the other hand Jung said the dream is an open message and is not distorted. Now, I don't think that is true and I think many of the dreams Jung interpreted he misinterpreted because they are not that open.

I have in the book *The Forgotten Language* (1951a) in the first place made one distinction between two kinds of symbols, namely the accidental symbol and the universal symbol. If I dream for instance about a city, about a house, about some particular time, then I deal with an accidental symbol, and only by the associations of the patient can I really know what it means; otherwise I couldn't know it. Take for instance the following dream:

> *Dream:* A person dreams that he is first in a big close building, then with a girl, but he is afraid that people will recognize him; then he finds himself with the girl on a beach, walking on the ocean but it is night, and in the third part of the dream he is all by himself, to the right of him are ruins and to the left of him are cliffs.

There you do not need associations necessarily because this dream deals in universal symbols. And what we find in this dream is a regression in depth. Consciously his level is that he is with the girl—the patient is married; he is in a big building, however, that is a mother symbol, but still he is with the girl, but he is frightened. Then he still is with the girl, but it is night, and eventually he is all alone and he is only with the mutilated mother, namely the cut off cliffs and ruins. Here you see in this dream the center problem of this patient formulated, without the necessity of understanding or even having association. (I ask every patient for associations because sometimes in this case the associations help—and I find many dreams where something essential is repressed.)

Considering that a dream is not only a open message but that there are many dreams where something of importance is repressed, Jung gave a very good example. In one dream he reports in his posthumously published autobiography (C. G. Jung, 1963), he dreamt:

> …that he felt he had to kill Siegfried. So he goes out and kills him. He feels very guilty and is afraid that he would be detected. To his great satisfaction comes a heavy rain which washes away all traces of the crime. He wakes up with the feeling: "I have to find out what this dream means otherwise I have to kill myself." He thinks about it and he finds out that the dream means that in killing Siegfried he kills the hero in himself and that the dream is a symbol of his own humility.

This dream was indeed distorted, because the name Sigmund (Freud) was changed into Siegfried. That was all the distortion there was. And that was enough for Jung, not to see that in this dream he was doing precisely what Freud had always told him he wanted to do, namely to kill him. He wasn't even aware of the meaning of something so simple, namely the feeling that if he did not understand the dream right, he would have to kill himself. What it really means, of course, is that if he did not misunderstand the dream correctly, namely his wish to kill Freud, he would have to kill himself. So he found an understanding which is the opposite of what the dream really means.

Here you see how there is distortion, how there is complete repression and then a rationalizing interpretation of the dream. That doesn't happen so rarely; that's why the Jungian version that the manifest text is always identical with what Freud called the latent content is simply not true.

In many ways what I call universal symbols are Jung's archetypes; it is only a little difficult to talk about Jung theoretically because he has expressed himself very brilliantly, but very often in a not quite clear fashion. It is also difficult to be sure what exactly he meant by any of his concepts. But nevertheless the concept of the archetype is a very fruitful concept. At least what it refers to is. One might also stress from a humanistic standpoint, that since man is always the same in his very basic condition of existence, namely in being split between awareness and being determined as an animal and yet having self-awareness, therefore man has only a few solutions, a few answers to give to the question which life poses to him. These answers can be regression to the mother's womb, it can be the answer of finding safety and obedience to the father; it can be the answer which has been the answer of the great religions and the humanist philosophies, namely of finding new harmony with the world by developing all his human powers, especially reason and love. In other words, the number of answers which man can give to the question of life are limited. He has to choose between them, and the number of symbols which represent these answers are also limited. They are universal, because there is only one man.

There are a few choices man can make. The concept of the symbol of the hero, for instance, symbolizes a man who dares to risk individuation. Or, as the Old Testament says, Abraham is a hero, because Abraham is told by God: "Leave thy country, leave thy father's house, and go to a country which I shall show you." [Ex 12:1] Always the symbol of the hero is a person who dares to risk his whole existence by independence and who is daring in this sense, who leaves certainty and risks uncertainty. That is in fact part of the fate of man, and that is one of the possibilities for man. The other possibility is precisely not to dare to risk individuation and to get stuck in mother, home, blood, soil, and never reach individuation and never become an independent person.

The question of when and how to tell the meaning of a dream to the patient depends on the situation. If the patient will tell me a dream in the second hour I will probably not say much because I will assume that if I would give him an interpretation he would not understand it. But there are also some people (even if they are not near psychosis) who are very sensitive and who like poetry, who would understand this interpretation because they are not bound so much to words and to concrete things. I might however even in the second hour say to the patient who dreamt of the big houses and ruins: "You seem to be afraid of being cut off from life and being stuck with something which is dead, ruinous which has no life," because that's precisely what the patient is.

How I use the dream depends on what I think the patient could understand at the moment. I am not so terribly cautious except with some patient who might not understand it. Many students in seminars, when they are presenting a case and I suggest they tell something to the patient, will say: "Well, but I am afraid the patient cannot take it." My first response usually is: "The only one who cannot take it is you, because you are afraid of sticking your neck out telling something to the patient, to which the patient might react with anger, with disturbance, and you are not sure that you are right—it is not a matter of being right necessarily—but you are not sufficiently sure of your own interpretation." To really sense the meaning of a dream, one needs a good deal of experience and sensitivity and what one calls "empathy."

9

Christiane: A Case History with Remarks on Therapeutic Method and on Understanding Dreams

The First Three Sessions and the First Dream

Reporter: This is a woman I started to see a year and a half ago. What I attempt to do is to take notes of the first three or four sessions. I usually don't make many notes after that because of dreams; I keep a record of dreams. I can tell you about the first few sessions and some of the family background and then some dreams.

Christiane is a 28-year-old woman, who is very attractive, well-dressed, very poised, sophisticated, sort of a formal-looking person, who has a very firm jaw but very dull eyes. She came in saying that she was very depressed the previous week when it was her fifth wedding anniversary. She got married at 23. That same week she also heard from a former boyfriend whom I'll call Uwe. He called and they spoke at some length. They each confessed that they still loved each other. She said right off in this context that her parents never approved of Uwe, who had artistic interests, mainly poetry. Rather her father admired her husband who was a graduate of a famous university.

She said she is very unhappy in her marriage, and this unhappiness took a new role last week. She mentioned it to her gynecologist whom she saw that week for her regular checkup. She also told him during this time that she had never had an orgasm. He spoke with her a while and gave her my name. So she called me; she had never thought of psychoanalysis before but felt it might be a good idea.

Although she is living what she calls "a good life"—that is, she has a very nice apartment, they have ample money, she has friends, and there's no flaw that she can point to—she finds herself very unhappy and sees no future in her marriage. Her husband, who is thirty, doesn't know that she's unhappy. He thinks they have a fine relationship. He relies on her to handle the details of living. If there's anything that goes wrong in the apartment, she's the one who calls the superintendent, and so forth, although they both work and she's not home during the day. But his main concern is focused on his business career. He is a manager. She describes him as being uptight and establishment-oriented and feels that he is that way in his work and at home.

Sadly, she says that they have sex rarely, maybe two or three times a month, but it's boring. He has trouble having an erection, so when they have intercourse he usually has an orgasm within a minute. She wonders if she should get a divorce but the very idea frightens her, because she knows that it would upset her parents greatly.

Christiane does personnel work for a large company and she earns fifteen thousand dollars a year. Later it turns out that she also has income from a trust fund of about that same amount. First she studied literature and graduated, then she changed universities and got a master's in economics. Now there's a little detail here. She changed to a university where she had some friends in that region, and first she applied for the graduate school studying literature, but she filled out an application in such a hurried way that it was very sloppy and she was not surprised when it was rejected. Then she re-applied for economics and was accepted there. Speaking of her study she is quiet, anxious, and rather little-girlish. She speaks like someone of eighteen or nineteen. She is distinctly uncomfortable and then doesn't know what to say, just that everything makes her unhappy. When I questioned her she said being with her daughter makes her happy. She has a daughter of one year who is taken care of during the day by a nursemaid. Otherwise, though she has many friends, she does nothing exciting and she has never felt, she says, any particular sense of joy in her whole life. She says "I feel confined like I'm in an emotional straitjacket. I was always a very conventional person."

Fromm: I would like to ask you a question: She mentioned first as the reason why she doesn't think of divorce that it would upset her family. Did she not mention the problem of the child? In a divorce she would probably keep the child because of its age, is that correct?

Reporter: That's correct. She does not feel that would be a problem at all, because she has enough money between her job and trust fund.

She said: "I was always very conventional until I met Uwe, when I was seventeen." In this context she said: "I once stayed out all night with him and my family was furious. It was the first time I ever rebelled. But I've always conformed ever since." Uwe is married and he lives in Düsseldorf and he called up from Düsseldorf. They had somehow kept in touch sporadically. From the time she was eighteen till twenty she and Uwe occasionally had intercourse. She enjoyed being with him, but nothing could come of that relationship.

Fromm: She was not frigid in this?

Reporter: She never had an orgasm, not even then. Well, in the past few days, before coming to the first session she had actually spoken to Uwe every day on the telephone, an hour, an hour and a half, something like that. She said if he lived nearby I'm sure we would have an affair. And then in desperation the night before, she told her husband that Uwe had called her long-distance from Düsseldorf, that's all she said. He shrugged his shoulders and made no comment about it.

Christiane said something is wrong in the marriage, but she said it was supposed to be a perfect match. "My father felt it was a very good marriage, as did my mother, and they always guided me in important decisions." Her father, she mentioned, is the president of a very large company and he heads up a major organization. She noticed at this point in the session, and she said: "You know I did have a dream this morning before coming, just before the session.":

> *Dream 1:* I am at a wedding and I have to be the maid of honor but I'm wearing a tailored dress instead of a proper gown like the others are wearing. And so I cannot perform my function.

Christiane said she had no idea what the dream meant except she doesn't like to feel out of place.

Fromm: We had heard about this woman, about the first three sessions. There's a woman of 28, who is unhappy—depressed is a physical term, unhappy is a human term. And one isn't quite sure here what is what. Anybody would be unhappy in fact to be married to a man whom she doesn't love, who doesn't love her, to be the prisoner of her parents, until the age of twenty-eight. Of never having done what she wanted but always what the parents wanted; how wouldn't she be unhappy? But she doesn't know why she's unhappy. She thinks she has an unhappy marriage.

I would just like to express this way of talking—most people talk that way today. They *have* an unhappy marriage; some people would still say they *have* a happy marriage. If anybody says "I *have* a happy marriage" you see that her marriage is not likely to be very happy. Because one cannot *have* an unhappy marriage, nor can one *have* a happy marriage. One can be happy with one's husband or one's wife, or one can be unhappy. But the marriage becomes a piece of property, an institution. I *have* that. Most people say today: "I *have* a problem," but they don't have a problem; maybe the problem has one.

What does it mean if one says: "I *have* a problem?" This is only a cover-expression with which one puts a state of mind in terms of a property relationship. In the same way I say, "I *have* a husband," "I *have* children," "I *have* a car," "I *have* a good marriage," "I *have* insomnia," instead of saying: "I cannot sleep." Everything is a noun which is connected with the word to have instead of to denote what one really means, a verb, namely "I cannot sleep," "I am unhappy," "I love," or "I don't love." This peculiar thing of speaking in terms of nouns which I have noted, instead of verbs, has been already mentioned in the eighteenth century. Dr. Chomsky called my attention to it by a writer, Du Marsais, who writes exactly about how wrongly people express feelings or states of being in terms of *having* something.

Of course if you say "I *have* an unhappy marriage," "I have a happy marriage"—what you do really is to protect yourself from experiencing something. This is because then it becomes many of the properties you have. Later on, Marx has talked about it when people speak about love instead of about loving. Love becomes a noun: "I have love;" "I give you love;" "the child didn't get enough love"—or as it's usually said—"much love." It reminds me of half a pound of cheese. What is "much love?" Either I love or I don't love. My love may be more intense, I may love more intensely, less intensely, but the whole concept of "much love," or the child didn't get "enough" love is the same as saying the child didn't get enough milk, or didn't get enough food. All this way of using nouns connected with *to have* is a way to protect oneself from experiencing.

I mention this here only as a footnote to Christiane reporting she *has* an unhappy marriage, or she *has* trouble in her marriage. What is marriage? Two people live together, they are legally married—that's the ceremony, but the marriage becomes here a thing, so it's happy or unhappy or good or bad and the experience, that which is personal, disappears.

I personally believe that in analysis it's very important to point out the language to the person who is analyzed, to point out what the function of this language is. This holds true not only in respect to the connection of nouns with *to have* but in many, many other respects. I don't mean analysis of language now in the sense of the British philosophical schools, but just to show what you are really saying, why you are putting things this way. It's very often as important a clue to what goes on in the other person as a dream. And it is very often eye-opening, because one can easily demonstrate this is something of an unconscious motivation which appears in the way a person expresses something.

To give an example: You find very often somebody saying "It seems I cannot do this." What does it mean "It seems I cannot do it?" To whom does it seem? Why does it seem? It really means "It seems that I cannot do it," that the person shrugs away his own responsibility. If he said "I believe I cannot do it," "I feel I cannot do it," then he would say something closer to reality. But he or she doesn't want to say this, because that is already revealing too much. He or she puts it on this very impersonal level "it seems." He or she might as well say "God believes I cannot do it," or "It is in the cards" or "in the stars" or "It is somewhere written in the book, in the laws of history that cannot do it." The formulation "it seems" may not represent something so deeply unconscious. It is usually more a figure of speech because this has something to do with the social character. All people use that same figure of speech because in our whole culture today we are accustomed to shove away things from the experience of *being*.

Christiane is not aware of this. She is only aware of the fact that she has an unhappy marriage and she is not aware of the fact that she is necessarily unhappy. For instance, it might be a good thing to tell her after an hour or two hours: "Well, I'm not surprised that you are unhappy, anybody would be." I remember once a writer from Hollywood came to me. He was quite a gifted writer and complained to me that his sense of creativity was waning. He felt he could not create anymore. And he told me his story in Hollywood and I said to him: "Well, with this life you lead nobody would have a sense of creativity. If you want to be creative you must become an honest man. If you go on living in that atmosphere you will never be able to do something with your talent which years ago, when you were not yet that poisoned, you could."

It is important to see for oneself and to show to people that when someone is unhappy, has this or that problem, this is nothing so mysterious, that it is not such a strange illness, but that is very often the totally logical consequences of an inner situation combined with an outer situation which would create certain symptoms just as in certain food; a certain unhealthy diet would create certain physical symptoms. And there is no mystery about it. Of course it is also important to demystify all these processes as much as one can. That means also to take away the belief that these are strange things for which one necessarily needs a specialist.

People have lived for hundreds of years and have coped with their problems just as well or better, long before psychoanalysis was discovered as a science. It is true enough that psychoanalysis, if properly applied, can really do a great deal to help people in expediting, intensifying a process which otherwise might not be so easy. Especially since in previous centuries when people were not yet so lost and without any instructions about behavior of life, people had much more sense of values, of goals, or aims, and therefore certain remedies, certain ideas, certain directions were given to them in their culture. Today we have nothing of that kind and therefore it seems as if by oneself one couldn't get anywhere.

I spoke about how Christiane has always stopped herself by a little compromise. The clearest thing about that was the application for graduate school in literature, where she goes instead to the school of economy because that's what the parents thought best. And then we saw her relationship to her father, in which there is a deep attachment. Of course we might ask here for a moment: How would a Freudian see Christiane?

From a Freudian point of view the answer would clearly be: This is the typical attachment of the daughter to the father, it has a sexual origin and what one can do about it, one can analyze early experiences, early sexual wishes, fantasies, and so on. Then the repressed incestuous wishes will come to the fore and if they do come to the fore then this attachment will dissolve itself because it has been brought to consciousness. The so-called patient will be free to turn her libido to men other than the father. The fixation will be solved. Well, that's one view.

From my standpoint, I would say it's quite normal that every little boy, being a boy, has already at an early age some erotic feeling, attachment for women, and vice versa as a girl. One isn't born as a neuter and Freud has discovered that this turns out to be true not only at the same age, at puberty, but relatively early. We know also that in fact it's not just father and mother who are the objects of this incestuous striving, but Freud reports in his own cases—take the Little Hans and other cases—the little boy is just as interested in a little girl of his own age as he is in his mother. Any female will do and for the little girl vice versa. Of course the father is an impressive figure, but not primarily erotically or sexually.

Besides that, one would have to say, generally speaking, sexual attraction and infatuation are notoriously fickle. That is to say, we see that in adult life. If two people are attracted to each other on purely sexual grounds, that is to say where sex as such remains the bond, and assuming nothing else happens, well, the estimates vary how long that lasts, but I would say a conservative estimate is about six months. It may be a little longer or much shorter. From a standpoint of deep, lasting bonds to another person, that's another thing. Sex is the least lasting thing, the least binding thing. I should like to make one exception just to express myself most correctly: with the exception of very peculiar perversions. If two people find each other, let us say, in extreme sadism and extreme masochism, and their perversions fit each other so completely that they could rarely find another person with the same peculiar tastes, then such sexual bonds in themselves last often for a long time. But this is not the rule. So the whole idea that this early sexual attraction to a father or a mother should last until one is fifteen is rather against all evidence about the effect of sexual bonds *per se*.

What does have a tremendous influence is the affective bond. Here mother gives shelter, protection, admiration, is, if you like, the earth, nature, where one belongs, where one has a home, who never leaves one, who loves one unconditionally. The father is for the little girl the admirable man who has other functions than the mother: he is kind, he teaches her things, and so on.

I would say it is not to be expected that our knowledge about early sexual attractions will contribute much to the understanding of this. By that I do not mean to say that one should not explore them, because one might always find that there is something special that is repressed—let us say the father may have tried to seduce the little girl, or the mother, in her own way, the little boy. These seductions are not so rare; they are different actually according to social class. The number of cases in which let us say peasants sleep with their daughters when they are more or less old enough, is relatively large. In the higher classes this is usually not done. The men find, if you like, the image of a young girl in women who can be bought for this purpose and they find sufficient and subtle ways to seduce the daughter to bind her affectively to him without any overt, or too overt, sexual element.

I don't mean to say one should eliminate the question of early sexual attachment, but one shouldn't expect it: There is a great problem if we find out what sexual trauma there is, or what particular things from childhood with regard to sex will appear; then we will really know the secret. The secret is very simple. Christiane, like anyone else, needs affection, needs protection, needs somebody to teach her, someone to direct her, who orients her, who praises her, who has a feeling of warmth towards her. The father is the given person for that, especially when the mother is as cold and narcissistic as Christiane's mother is. There is nobody else in this family by whom she could get some sense of a personal tie or of any kind of personal concern.

The father is too abstracted to give much, but apparently he has some, and so Christiane, who grows up in fear of the mother and in the fear that if she doesn't do the right thing then the father will cease to love her, this girl lives under a constant blackmail. The only thing she has, namely this father's love, will disappear if she doesn't behave. But she has so far been so blackmailed, so frightened, so intimidated, so far from thinking that she could do something with her own life, so little adventurous, that she is still willing to lie down and not to assert herself and not to live her own life and to find somebody whom she could love. Uwe she was in love with before he would be possibly the one whom she seems to be in love with at the moment (when psychotherapy started), although one cannot really at this point of the argument know how serious that is. But simply by contrast to the husband, Uwe is a lovable man. So far as this constellation is, there's nothing extraordinary about it. We can see here, in the first three hours she has not caught on too well to the analytic procedure. She has been defensive, she has made this little step of separating from the husband so that she can prove to herself that she doesn't need anything more, and here's where Uwe came in.

The first dream says she was wearing at the wedding a tailored dress. It was the dream that she shouldn't be married really, that her wedding shouldn't have taken place. The fact that in the dream her function was to be the maid of honor I wouldn't make too much of it because of the following understanding. In each dream there is a scene like in a plot. I mean each dream is a short play of which the dreamer is the director, the actor, and the author. One can only see a dream as a play which is arranged by the dreamer; he could have dreamt anything else but each play has its own logic. Once I invent this plot, the plot itself has its own logic. Very often it is not necessary or not even particularly fruitful to discuss every detail, inasmuch as the detail is part of the plot. If Christiane has chosen to disguise her wedding by the situation of being the maid of honor, well, that is one of the ways in which one disguises the wedding, that's the social pattern, and we must not forget in the dream the censor operates. Even in her dream she is very little free and so she censors that out.

In fact, to say something in general, I think each dream has a maximal interpretation and an optimal interpretation, by which I mean you can interpret a dream maximally, that is to say you take every piece, every little thing and want to know what does it mean. I am much more in favor of the optimal interpretation; that is to say, to interpret the most important message of the dream. Once one has got that to say there are many other little details, but if I look for all these details at the same time I am losing often what is the impact of the central message of the dream. Because a dream is a message, you might say, of the dreamer to himself, and sometimes a message also to the analyst, and sometimes to another person to whom one may tell the dream. So I'm more prone—as long as a part of the dream fits into the chosen plot—not to interpret too much, because one gets overcrowded.

Usually I ask the person whom I analyze what he or she thinks about the dream. Then I would ask what associations he or she has about the dream because sometimes associations are important; very often they are not necessary. I would say about fifty percent of all dreams you can understand without associations, because they are written in symbolic language; they are perfectly clear. Freud in his dream interpretation only relies on associations; the piece of a dream has significance only inasmuch as he has associations to it, and then the real piece, the manifest piece is replaced by an association, another association, then the next and the next, and you get a mountain of associations to one manifest piece, and very often the meaning of the dream is completely lost.

Actually there is great ingenuity in Freud's dream interpretation, but I would say if you have finished reading a dream in Freud's interpretation you hardly know more about the patient than you did before. You have heard a brilliant firework about hundreds of associations but then you might ask what do I know about the patient, the unconscious feelings, what moves the patient—nothing more. But Freud has really opened the way to see beneath the dream, to see the dream as something meaningful. Yet his own method of interpreting I think was very misleading, and that is because of one quality of Freud: Freud had no real sense for symbolism, as he had no sense for art and poetry, he had a sense for that only which one could conceive intellectually. I think it was Glover in England who said: "If I don't see the associations as well as the patient, I don't know any more about him than somebody who is not a psychoanalyst."

Any direct impression from what comes over from another person by the voice, the gesture, the face, the body attitude, but then also by the subtlety of the nuances in which he expresses himself, is lost. In fact, somebody who is not as insensitive to the life of the patient as Freud was would not have invented a method to sit behind him and not to see him, denying himself the most important source for understanding another person. Naturally if you don't see the face, you miss a great deal of what is essential for the knowledge of the other person.

The Second Month of Therapy and the Second Dream

Reporter: After the third week she had decided to leave the marriage and to separate from her husband. There was then a period of a few weeks when he had a great deal of difficulty in coming to terms with this. But once the decision was made and he decided to move out, he first made an attempt to find an apartment in the same building. Christiane actively protested; thus he moved out to a hotel not far away. In that particular period of time she cried in nearly every session. She would come in with a sort of brave but thin smile and then quickly break into tears. During that time she would telephone me during the day and night at least one or two times a day. She said she was absolutely frightened to leave but she said "it is urgent that I do." She was absolutely terrified of being alone. We discussed this. It was queer that never in her life had she really been alone. She was with her family till the ninth grade, then in a highly structured private school, in a structured college setting, in a structured post-graduate setting, and then she got married. She had never lived alone. This would be the first time she ever ventured forth on her own two feet.

During this time, the second month of therapy, she spoke largely of her family. She said in her family group behavior was absolutely required, no one was permitted to show anger; sadness was not allowed. One always had to put forth a good face no matter how one felt. Even when she had her piano lessons which she did for years, from around the age of 10 to 14, her mother would lock her in her room each day to practice. It was simply part of the procedure to go in and you're locked in, and the patient never questioned it; nor was she aware during this time of having ever experienced any anger at her mother. She simply took this for granted. Also when she told this she felt no anger. When I said: "You say this in a remarkably calm way," she answered: "Why, that's just how it was."

Her father was held up to her as a god, but was sentimental and more understanding than mother. Mother never had anything personal to do with her. However, on many a Saturday afternoon father would read children's stories. I don't recall which stories, but when she was five, six, seven, eight, he would take an hour on Saturday afternoon when he was at home, and read stories to her and to her friends, so there'd be four, five, six girls to whom he would read. And apparently he did this with a certain gusto.

In the third month of therapy her boyfriend Uwe came to visit. He came from Düsseldorf to Frankfurt while her husband was out of the house. Uwe and Christiane slept together. They did this several times. It was very stimulating, very exciting. She still did not have an orgasm, but she was so happy to be with somebody because she'd been so frightened of being alone. Uwe told her that he was still committed to his wife and he doesn't see how they could really get married. This he told her after he'd slept with her. The intercourse reduced her anxiety level, because she was from time to time on the verge of panic, very frightened. There were some extra sessions during that time and many phone calls. During this time she got quite dismayed; she expressed frequent despair that things would not improve. She had left her husband, but nothing really changed. She still felt very lonely and felt nothing basically would ever change. I spoke about her fear of being alone and abandoned and discussed with her the type of fear of being abandoned as if she was still a child completely dependent on her parents.

Fromm: Although I am quibbling here with words which I don't mean to say, but just this "as if…" is of course not correct, because she *is* still a child, dependent on her parents. She *is* a three-year-old child. She *is* that. The fact that she has a biological age of twenty-eight and that she might make a jump from three to twenty-nine, if I would be radical I would say "in a minute," that's something else. But at this point she is a child. That has a certain importance because as long as I say to somebody "You act as if you were a child," this is a kind of friendly censor: "Don't be so childish." If I say: "You *are* a child of three years of age"— this is a much more shocking remark because it is much more near to the truth and it's not such a conventional thing. The conventional thing is "You are as if you were a child." But this "as if" is only a half-truth. She *is* a child—and that is a shocking fact to which she must wake up, and therefore anything that tends to make this, play this down, by the "as if" diminishes the significance of the statement you make.

That of course has to do in general with a style of talking to the person one analyzes about which I wanted to talk in general because it's a very complex problem. It is of course, you might say, much more daring to say to a twenty-year-old person "You *are* a child of three" because it sounds like a great insult to say that. But in fact the patient knows that that *is* so and it depends entirely upon how it is said. It could be said in a critical way and then it may be devastating. But once the patient has realized that the therapist is not out to criticize her but to help her, then the same statement might be extremely helpful by its shocking nature because the other person has known that for a long time, but not being fully aware of it. She is greatly relieved that the analyst sees that too, and takes it for granted, while she has had this as one of her most terrible secrets—this feeling I am still a little child, although she did not phrase it in these terms.

The purpose is not only to convey to the patient that while she felt as a child of three, she at the same time was carrying over the experience of three-year-oldness to the present time when her life is not dependent for survival on her parents. This is a very good rationale, but you have to speak as closely to the reality that this person is feeling as possible, that is to say, closer to the feelings of fear on a deeper level. In the deeper level of fear, no "as if" exists, because to add "ifs" is already a rational category. Christiane knows she feels that she is a child and she is *frightened* and doesn't dare to be aware of it.

Reporter: At this time Christiane had another dream which she broke down and brought in:

> *Dream 2:* It was a few days before my wedding and several close girlfriends were house-guests. We decided to go swimming at a pool nearby, but it was an anxious time. Some girls wanted to

> go and others wanted to sit around the house. I put on my bathing suit but I didn't know what suit I had put on. One of the girls commented that it was an old-fashioned suit and it was also old in age. It was yellow, and it covered almost my whole body. It's the kind of bathing suit my mother wears. I looked for my bikini in my closet but I couldn't find it. Everyone was in a hurry so I had to leave without the bikini and I wore the old suit. The pool was great and everyone was happy. I anticipated the wedding and was exhilarated. Suddenly the dream shifted to a sickbed where Martha, my old housekeeper (the one who brought her up) was very sick and dying. She had a bad disease where all her insides were coming out; it was very upsetting but my mother did not seem to mind and took the entire experience in a matter-of-fact way. It was very upsetting to me, as I realized my mother didn't care about Martha.

My reaction to the dream had something to do with her recognition that her mother, while giving lip-service to being interested in people and in Christiane, really didn't have that kind of interest, that she was very absorbed in her own affairs. Something of that sort. Christiane herself again had no thought for associations about the dream.

Fromm: This impression doesn't take care of the first part of the dream. In the first part she really feels before everything, she is her mother, or we might say she feels she's forced to be her mother. Here the paradox appears. While she is going to marry, which means to be a woman in her own right, with her own life, the dream tells her, symbolized in the dresses, that she has to be like mother, or she has to be mother, she has to obey her, she is bound. She is forced, so to speak, to wear the mother's uniform. In this period she marries, and this is a perfectly good description; she marries a man mother forces her to wear. So what she is really telling herself or what she is really expressing is: "I married not as I, but as my mother. I married this man because my mother made me marry him." She did not marry as a free woman, or of her free choice, or of any feeling of herself. And then she contrasts this with a critical thought about her mother: that her mother is utterly indifferent to any human. In these two parts, on two different levels of symbolism, she says: "I had to marry this man against my wishes, because my mother doesn't care the slightest bit about any other human being, including myself, and so I married him." This thought is expressed in these two dream parts.

I want to mention here one important problem of analytic procedure. There comes a point where one can speak in two different ways. The analyst can say: "That's what you feel. You feel your mother is this, this, or this." Or the analyst can say "That's what you feel and you're damned right. This is so." That makes a great deal of difference, because this woman doesn't dare to think that what she feels is right, that she has any right to do it, this is *lese majesty*, this is something terrible, to feel that about her mother. Only in her dreams does she dare to express that, not in reality. Now, if the analyst says: "You are wrong, this is so, your mother *is* almost a monster"—that indeed is a completely new experience, because for the first time she dares to think that her own impression, her own thoughts are right thoughts which in her life she had never dared to tell anybody, including herself.

Another question is: There are two different parts in the dream. Do these two parts necessarily belong together in analyzation? Out of methodological reasons I would say there is nothing which is necessarily so. All these interpretations depend on the experience of the interpreter of the dream and they depend on the clarity of the dream. From my experience, I would say most two-part dreams in one night form a unit and have the great advantage that very often they interpret each other. The one adds to the other, and it is indeed amazing how a person who otherwise when asked couldn't write three sentences of a novel, of a poem, in his or her sleep is capable of formulating an idea in symbolic language, so precisely, so beautifully, so artistically. Most of us do that in our dreams. Christiane chooses here a two-play which matches beautifully. She just uses two acts and that also helps the process of disguise. This is the main advantage of this from the standpoint of the dreamer; by dreaming these two different things in different symbolism she disguises better to herself, what should not be, what should not come to her consciousness.

This dream is also a classic expression of a fantastic phenomenon which I cannot help wonder at, although I have been concerned with dreams God knows how many years: how a person knows everything without being aware of it consciously. How in our sleep we know things although we disguise them. Christiane's dream shows clearly she knows all this, and yet in waking life she does deny this and nothing of this knowledge is available. And that is indeed why our dreams are so much more real than our waking thoughts. Our waking thoughts are mostly lies and fictions. To express myself somewhat more strongly for clarity's sake, I prefer to say most of our conscious thoughts are lies and fictions than to say most of our conscious thoughts are respectable and true.

In the second part of the second dream Christiane contrasts the role of her mother with the role of Martha, who brought her up. I don't think that these both are contrasting elements of Christiane. She dramatizes her mother. She says this woman has not a bit of feeling, and she puts in evidence a woman whom she really loves apparently and who cares for her, and that this mother is absolutely callous in respect to the one woman in her life. You might say the dream implies: If I were that sick (as Martha is) my mother wouldn't care much.

To think that the description of the illness where the insides were oozing out is a symbol for exposing one's feelings I would say is an over-interpretation of the second part of the dream. In this case the dream would be saying that the mother believed that exposing one's feelings is deadly. This in my opinion would be a kind of overinterpretation. It's theoretically possible but here comes an empirical factor which is a matter really of experience. Many interpretations are possible but one develops most in practice, a certain sense of what nevertheless is likely to be the meaning here. I feel this is a construction because—and this is very hard to prove—here the emphasis is on the suffering, on the severity of the disease. That is really expressed in this. That the oozing of the insides should at the same time have a reference to showing her feelings, speaking about this old woman, doesn't feel quite real. But theoretically it's a perfectly possible interpretation.

Here comes a great question, in general dream interpretation, of where to stick so closely to the material. The dream is so rich in what it describes as an expression of human feelings, that my preference is to stick so closely to what one can see immediately without theoretic construction and forget about that which one could construct because it wouldn't add anything either. We already know that she is afraid of that.

The Following Months and the Third Dream

Reporter: During this time a number of subtle changes did take place. First of all she began speaking about aspects of her life other than her family. She'd been troubled about her work situation, particularly the man that she worked for was sometimes a very authoritarian person who structured her situation rather a lot, and she felt often very confined by this situation. After some discussion about this, she decided she was able to speak to the boss higher up and discuss a transfer, a promotion. She also felt she had been underpaid and was capable of doing more interesting work. With some trepidation she was able to do this and within a very short time was promoted to a different division. Christiane was now out of personnel and into an executive management job where she would be in charge of some forty to fifty people. At this time she was so pleased about this that she called up her family and she briefed her mother, who naturally raised questions about the advisability of going into this different kind of work. Her father, however, said: "Well, this is excellent. You are moving from a staff position to a line position which is very good in your training in business." And with that she accepted this promotion and was very pleased to do so. And she really enjoyed the work. At the same time she gave up this brief relationship with Uwe, as she felt that it was not going to lead anywhere and why get caught up in it, although she knew that she would be in a position of great anxiety. This was something too that we did discuss. However, no sooner did she leave the situation with Uwe—or a few weeks later—she became involved with Peter, who was the father's big executive.

During this period of time though, prior to Peter, she did begin to think in more an analytic idiom, was very interested in discussing situations, and began to have some insights and interpretations of her own and became quite motivated.

Peter had kept in contact with her on his frequent flights from Hamburg to Frankfurt. After she had broken up with Uwe he had asked her before to go out to dinner—she finally accepted. She was a little concerned to accept because she knew she was very vulnerable and desperately wanted company. She did feel, and was in touch with a great deal of anxiety about being alone. For a few weeks she was busy every night going to one friend's house after another. That bored her, and then she began to take up the guitar.

With Peter she then had an affair, and she would see him about once a week. Within a month or so she and Peter fell very much in love with each other. They considered themselves to be in love. Peter is married and has three children. He is one of four vice-presidents in her father's organization. Peter knew that one of the vice-presidents is going to succeed the father when he gives up the chairmanship of this vast corporation. After about two months they became extremely close. Peter made several trips a week into Frankfurt and finally it got so hot and heavy and passionate that she felt that the family ought to know, because one way or another they were going to find out.

Christiane asked Peter whether the family should know. Peter was then deeply involved with her and said: "I don't think we should tell them everything, but tell them about our seeing each other." She spoke to her family about that they were seeing each other casually and rather liked each other. The parents got quite upset. They said: "Look, if something should happen here you're making a terrible error. He's married, he's got a family, he's got a future and he's certainly not for you."

After that conversation Christiane had the following dream:

> *Dream 3:* I was on a beach. There were no people around and I was very happy to be in a quiet, sunny place. I felt no tension, a complete escape. Then suddenly some authority figure (she doesn't know whether it was a man or a woman) told me that I had to organize an event that same afternoon. I didn't know what kind of event but I had to get off the beach and to get going. I don't know why I agreed. I met some friends, two childhood girlfriends. They said: "Don't worry, you can do it, and we'll be there. It'll be O.K." I didn't think they took it seriously enough. Then we were in a parish hall, in the church hall of my home town. I was looking at the stage in the parish hall. Next the scene changed. I was in the yard at our home. There were lots of trucks around, and a circus tent. And lots of musical instruments gathered about. I thought it was to be a play that I was to organize, as I had in high school. But instead I was to perform and I didn't know what to perform. I was very anxious. Someone said: "You are to dance here" on this red merry-go-round. There was a red merry-go-round with royal blue elephants with red seats all around—much room. At first I was glad to dance but not with such constraint.

Reporter: I said to her that here she had a sense of freedom, of doing something on her own, but nevertheless her parental influence carries over and she feels obligated to perform and to go on with the parental dictates. She does not feel free to follow through.

Christiane was still very frightened, she was absolutely frightened to continue with Peter, because she felt that this would be the end of everything. She would be guilty for Peter's lack of getting a promotion, maybe he'd be fired, and certainly she would incur the extreme wrath of her parents. She said when they get angry there is just no way to deal with them because they convey to her that she is not just bad but she is a disappointment to them. She says: "I always have to live in such a way as to make my mother's life feasible." Whenever she expressed happiness, her mother seemed to be unhappy. Or whenever she would do something that would get her more into the world, or threaten to, the mother was very dismayed and would convey a look of wretchedness: "Look what you're doing!"

Fromm: I just want to discuss the meaning of this whole story a little bit more. What goes on here? First of all one has certain questions: What does Peter think? Has he a secret scheme—eventually he will get a divorce, marry that girl, and thereby become president? That's not so far-fetched. It's rather a game with high stakes, because in the meantime in the process he might be thrown out. But otherwise: Why would Peter risk losing his job and why would Peter be so naive to think that eventually these people will not notice anything when the girl tells them that he is seeing her frequently? There is a funny thing: the naivety of these parents. Just because they care so little, they are so naive. If the daughter suddenly comes and says she sees Peter often, well, I guess anyone with half normal intelligence would say: obviously they are starting an affair, otherwise why would she come and tell this. That's a cover story that she sees him often. But these people take that very seriously and only threaten her with what would happen if she did.

I want to point out one thing here: that very often what one would call naivete or a strange kind of ignorance, is simply the result of caring too little. For these people the whole life of their daughter and what she does and what affairs she has is really not that important so they don't try enough to see what that really means, but are satisfied with some stupid cover story and leave it at that. Such parents are very easily deceived and their having her for twenty years meant simply nothing. In this twenty years obviously she did not experience enough which would make her feel that there she was really at home, and that gave her a deep sense of I don't know what, of at least being at home. These people then are so surprised when children suddenly do something unexpected because it's so in their minds that the children live for their sake and don't want to disappoint them, that they don't think of the possibility that their children are alive and might do something which they want to do, even if it sounds crazy or whatever, if it's something extreme they do, and so they don't notice anything. The same holds true very often in marriages. I remember a woman who was married for thirty years and didn't notice at all that the man was just driven to distraction.

If one sees instances of what one would call naivete, or lack of judgment, it's always very important not to talk about the lack of judgment, but to ask oneself: Are they not simply too disinterested to know better? I am sure you can show that the same people who are so naive with regard to their daughter's life are by no means so naive with their own affairs. This father would not be naive in the slightest about what's going on in his company. When an employee comes to him with a story in reference to something in the company—he would notice immediately that this is a cover story. But when his daughter comes he doesn't want to be bothered, he doesn't want to be drawn into conflict, so he believes her.

That the woman is driven to despair and anxiety is very clear, because what is all this? Peter told her only he was contemplating to leave his children and his wife. As long as he only contemplates it's just so much talk. If a man doesn't say "I shall, if you marry me, get a divorce immediately," it's not worth listening to it. And the trouble is that some women—and it's usually the women who are in that position—are so infatuated or don't see the man subjectively, who are so romantic that they don't see the reality, and really believe the man says he's going to contemplate it as if that means anything. It takes really some experience in living to become what I would say is normally, healthily cynical. I would recommend to everybody to become healthily cynical. It makes life much clearer, protects one from many errors, and means that one doesn't fall for all the sentimental well-meant swindles, for which people deceive each other and deceive themselves.

If you hear the story that these two people are so madly in love with each other, I'm not impressed. So what? He's lonely, she's lonely, so they are in love with each other. What does it all mean? What substance is there to that? What reality is there to that? He has in mind probably mainly his job and he is in a conflict and he's rather foolish, I should say. Why is he foolish? What is his calculation in this? I would be very interested to know because the man has something at stake here, and what his calculation is I don't know. But obviously he's not too serious, otherwise he would talk differently. Maybe he just plays with a high risk.

Christiane's own feeling in this is one of being completely bewildered. Again I would say: "Of course you're bewildered and anxious, because you're in an impossible situation. You are frightened of your parents. So far this man has given no indication that he really loves you in more than just a sense of going to bed with you and being very attracted to you at the moment. What basis is that for a relationship? How serious is it? You are twenty-eight." If she were seventeen or eighteen one might say alright. So she experiments and maybe there's no great harm in that, but it's a little late. (Although these are really muddy situations, I wouldn't even recommend them for the seventeen- or eighteen-year-old.)

The situation with this man is a muddy situation. It's basically dishonest. Why get oneself in a situation which is so basically dishonest? It's not necessary and it doesn't help anyone. It just leads to great disappointment and to the kind of cynicism which one shouldn't have. I think cynicism should be an accompaniment of great faith, but cynicism without faith is just discouragement, is just self-destructive. The question would be to know what does the girl—I say the girl (to say the "child," would be the most proper expression here)—what does the woman really say about that?

Reporter: She says that for the first time in her life she is now having orgasms. He claims it is the finest relationship he's had, the most powerful and sensuous.—I said to her that she is still frightened about being on her own. As soon as she could, she tried to take up with Uwe again. When that didn't work out again she was so frightened she latched on to Peter. And that she's still struggling without knowing what she's going to do, but it's mostly concerned with these different kinds of security operations to tie up with people who are going to give her that kind of security where she won't be drifting or on her own.

Fromm: One should, however, not take the fact too lightly; that she has an orgasm with this man is also not to be completely ignored. Whatever the reasons are—maybe this ban is of, less inhibitive, a better lover and has a different kind of temperament—she is freer. It's strange that in this case, which is most complicated from the standpoint of the parental situation, she really plays with fire. There she is less inhibited, can let herself go more than in situations which were actually less difficult. Especially with her husband it would be completely safe, but he gives no chance so we can forget about that. But also with Uwe. Thus I would say this is a symptom which I would take as an indication that she has still made no progress in essential things, respectively; this is at least something which is worthwhile to be enquired. Is there actually, in relationship to her parents, any change, basically, in these four months?

Reporter: Yes, there is a slight change in that she has become a little more skeptical about what they're like and about what their interest is in her. Her father, he calls her once or twice a week. Usually he is off to one of the branches every now and then and travels quite a bit. Returning to Frankfurt he calls her up, or he may see her for dinner every two or three weeks. She feels that he really is kind of superficial. She sees him in a less godlike way and begins to express a slight hostility towards her mother, in the sense of seeing the mother more clearly as someone who has subordinated her by putting the mother's own interests first. So there is a slight change in her view of the family, though in terms of her apprehension and fear, that still remains unchanged. She's still terribly frightened for some reason that they are simply going to abandon her.

Fromm: We might say on the other hand she still is having a life of her own, that is to say, being a three-year-old without a life of her own she is naturally afraid that the people who give some meaning to her life when she is at home could abandon her. Still she feels frightened to death of being left by her parents and we might say this is the result also of her not knowing anything about how to live, how to be, how to be a person. She goes to her job, that's a pretty routine thing, and then she flounders. She goes to her analysis. That must be to her one place where she has a little home, and then she sleeps with that man and that gives her a little feeling of being at home. But by and large this woman is completely without a sense that she *is*, that she is a person on her own, that she could do something, that she could live. She just flounders around completely.

Naturally you might say it goes both ways. One can argue: Because she is so bound to her parents she cannot think of her own life—that would be the usual analytic version. I think, however, you must say also it goes the other way around just as much or more, because she doesn't know anything about living. She does not feel anything she can do with her life, she is completely blind to what life could mean. She *has* to remain frightened as long as she has no vision. I don't mean a theoretical vision, I mean some feeling that here is life, it's her own, and that in this life she can do something, express something, be herself.

Here we come to a great problem: Is analysis enough? Or is it not necessary that somebody who explores himself or herself also learns how to live, that is to say, some idea of what one does with one's life. This woman is like a traveller in a desert without a map. She looks out for somebody who might come and show her out of the desert because she is frightened of dying from thirst. That is literally so, that is not a metaphor. She needs a map and the map is not only to see that she is dependent in all this, but the map is also to see now where could she go. What is this thing "life?" Who is she? What could she do? And with this I don't mean in practical terms of a job. Still we haven't asked what interests she has?

Reporter: She has a great deal of interest in music. She loves music of all kinds, but she doesn't play an instrument. However, at this time she felt she wanted to give some expression to music. She has always liked the guitar and began taking guitar lessons—not so much popular guitar, but to learn guitar as an instrument perhaps with a classical or opera guitar.

Fromm: When she says she has very much interest in music—let's forget about the guitar for a moment—what does she really mean? How is that evidenced?

Reporter: It is evidenced in the fact that she does go to the opera, and can get tickets to the Frankfurt Opera. I think it is not really out of status feeling or things to do. She genuinely enjoys opera. And she knows something about opera, the stories, the composers. Although this is not something I know much about, nevertheless I felt from the remarks she made she is more than a pure amateur.

Fromm: I must say that data doesn't impress me at all. Whether "one goes to the opera" in itself is the expression of a great interest in music, seems to me questionable, especially in Frankfurt where it's definitely a status thing. That's not very convincing to me. When somebody tells me he is very much interested in music, my next question is: "Please, tell me one piece that you like best?" It's an obvious question because only then can I have any idea what this means, and if the answer is "Well, I like everything" then I know: this statement about an interest in music is just a cliche. Besides that, we know how many people go to listen to music and go to museums. I'm sure quite a few are really interested, but you know today, everybody tries to kill time in the most decent way, if he belongs to certain educated classes. So you go and look at modern—or not modern—art, or to concerts, but this essentially isn't an expression of great interest in art, it's a conventional thing. So somebody will have to be more convincing than saying she goes to the opera.

She thinks that music is important to her, but I'm very skeptical in general towards these statements. What does it mean, that she is taking guitar lessons? In many cases that would be just one way of killing time. I don't think that's necessarily an expression of great musical interest. Like the older generation used to learn the piano. I don't know how conventional it is now to learn the guitar.

Reporter: I didn't feel it's the way she was involved in it, but I thought in the context of where she is in her life, that when she wants to get to play the guitar, even if it's a trivial interest, it's a desire to express some of her emotional reactions, just as was her going back to horseback riding, which she would do several mornings a week and on weekends. Again it may be to keep her busy, but it is something that gives her much pleasure, and actually horseback riding is an experience with nature and it has been her first love, in effect.

Fromm: She always loved horseback riding. That's a very sound and very pleasant experience and it shows she is not dead, but it doesn't show too much, that she takes something in this field seriously. As she doesn't report on her reading, I guess it is not a subject matter about which she gets very excited and a little enamored at each session, that she comes and talks for an hour about the books she has read. It's very interesting in general that so many people talk about what I would call very often banalities: so what did the boyfriend say, what did she do, and this and that and that which repeats itself, but they usually are not excited by anything which is outside of the strictly banal sphere of relatively meaningless personal events. With regard to Christiane we have to ask: This woman was once very interested in studying literature. The parents did a good job; now she seems not to be terribly interested in that anymore. So the one thing where she had a real interest apparently has been lost. She leads a life which is really in a way "barbaric"; by this I mean it has no content beyond that which concerns a narrow circle, of her job and her relation to her parents, with a few feeble attempts to branch out which gets her into great trouble.

The question is what can one do about that and what can analysis do about that—or should it? As long as she is so poor in terms of experiences which are fruitful and interesting in life, how can she build up a life which is not utterly boring? How can she leave this dependency on her parents? That is I would think a very important topic to be brought in and in my opinion in general analysis, too little attention is paid to it because it doesn't seem to be a problem or too little of a problem. If in the wealth of culture we live in and the wealth of possibilities with books and experience in science and everything a person lives as if all that did not exist, as if there was an empty world in which nothing is important, nothing is really interesting except purely small personal events.

The Fourth Dream and Some General Consideration about this Therapy

Reporter: The next dream marks the low point of our work together. It took place about a month later. What happened in the meantime was as follows. Discussing with Peter their greater involvement, they were now seeing each other about three times a week. Peter was travelling to Frankfurt much more than necessary and he could justify. Finally they decided they would tell the parents. Peter at this point did begin to feel that he did love Christiane. He definitely said that it was not only a commonplace but he told her very seriously that maybe they could work out a life together, but he would only do so if he felt that he could also manage his career. He felt that that was very important and he didn't want to feel that he would give it up for her. Christiane said she didn't want him to give it up for her.

But Christiane felt that perhaps with her father, who had said he would stand by her no matter what, possibly under the circumstances they might go along with it. She then made arrangements to fly to Hamburg and she spoke to her family, to both parents together. The parents reacted with extreme dismay; in fact they acted very angrily. They thought "How could you do this?"

Fromm: If I may say this between: that was particularly a mistake of hers, she should have talked to her father separately first. In the presence of the mother this was already a losing battle.

Reporter: Then her father the next day spoke with Peter, and Peter said to the father—as both people reported to Christiane later—spoke very directly. Peter said: "I love Christiane and I would like to marry her. My marriage has not been a very good one. . . ." Thus he declared his intentions. The parents had a consultation, and the next day, it was a Sunday, they met with Peter and with Christiane, and they said: "Look, we simply cannot go along with this. The organization would be scandalized, it would absolutely jeopardize your future, you couldn't possibly get ahead, and I don't know that it would be comfortable given the social situation in which we all live, that you could stay here." The parents declared themselves, jointly, totally against this match. The father said to Peter, as a matter of fact, that he will be fired unless he agrees to the following compromise. The compromise was that they not speak to each other for one year. If at the end of that one year of not speaking with each other, they would still feel strongly, they could re-address their petition, as it were, to the family.

For Christiane this was no laughing matter. After she came back to Frankfurt—it was Sunday night—I saw her Monday morning. She had had the following dream that night. It was for her the most serious dream she'd ever had:

> *Dream 4:* I am in a room which is a meeting room. I am up on stage with about twelve other men and women. Someone is running the meeting like a trial by vote. We twelve have been accused of some disloyalty, nothing definite. We indeed are accused and our punishment is death, to be handled by injec-tions from a doctor. My parents are at the meeting and—Lisa that's the daughter—is with them. Henry (a kind of old friend that she has known on and off, he knows the family and is friendly to her) is not in the room but sitting in a nearby room that's like a press room, right next to the meeting hall. The hall is old, wooden and crude. It reminds her in some way of a church.

> We are going to die. The order that we will be killed has been determined and I am one of the last. First the people who have displayed leadership, mainly the men, are followed by the women, in the order in which they will be killed. I am not last because I displayed some leadership. The picture of order in which the twelve would be put to death was put up on a chart. Next to each name there were Ankh symbols. This is the Egyptian symbol of life. It goes like this: On this chart the Ankhs were upside-down but then turned forty-five degrees, thus the little circles look up. People had five, four, three, or two Ankhs. I had only two or three. That's like she was close to the bottom. The first to die had it easier than the rest of us who had to wait. Because they would have to see the others die. There was a room next to the stage where the doctor was, with a large couch, the kind you give blood on, only more stuffed. It was like the green

benches they sometimes have in the hospital where you lie down and give blood, but it was more of upholstered, stuffed. It was dark green. The entire dream was in colors of greens, browns, and greys.

The process of the death was first to have two large shots. First you get one and then you get a second one and finally after a while you got a third injection which would kill. Everyone in the room was politely nice and superficially sympathetic. My parents were kind but detached. They told me they would take care of Lisa. I would leave the room from time to time to see my friend Henry, but he was cold, not very sympathetic and he kept saying: "I told you so, that this would happen." He admonished me in a detached way. I wanted his love and closeness so much, but he wouldn't give. I had the two shots and then I took Lisa for a last walk. We went up and down a sidewalk which is near my office—a dark, dirty street. Lisa was dressed all in white lace, and in a beautiful white and navy blue baby carriage. I felt tremendous dread and fear, deep pain, but it wasn't strange that I never cried. I came back and looked in the mirror and I looked very chalky and pale and sort of dead. There were cries and whispers from the surroundings. People stood and talked, and finally my turn came again and as the doctor injected me for the third time, I woke up.

When we spoke about the dream her anxiety was enormous. By this treatment of her family she felt condemned to die, her parents were of no help to her in any way. They go along with the sentence and do nothing. She feels the doctor is not helping her but hurting her and felt no choice but to go along with the punishment that her parents and the facts had metered out. We discussed the question how is it that she's still so locked into, obedient to, and frightened of the parents.

Fromm: This dream could be a Kafkian story, exceedingly artful and deeply felt. Now here she sees her situation as a depth which only really a great poet, a great writer like Kafka, could put down on paper. She cannot put it down on paper but she is able to express this with a great accuracy, intensity of feeling, with great beauty, the whole lot. The dream hardly needs any comment. This is a situation where she feels she is completely beaten, she is at the end. It is as a reaction to her parents' reaction, it is the feeling now she has lost. Finally there is nowhere to go. Here comes something where she puts the analyst together with the parents. She doesn't just say: "He hasn't helped me," but he is playing the role with the parents together. That is to say, she has not put the analyst as a figure against her parents but she puts the analyst as another figure together with her parents. The question is whether that could have been avoided, by a more active and a more direct partner- ship, as it were, against the parents.

In such a situation I would make very clear how I experience these parents: the mother inhuman and the father as a weak, ineffective man as far as human relationships are concerned. I would make clear that I find it shocking that they have pressured to a point that she doesn't dare to feel this anymore. Let me put it this way: Every real growing up is an act of revolution, of a personal revolution. It means freeing oneself from the people who want to run one's life. Whether they want to run it openly or whether they want to run it smoothly, it's in every case, every person's development, to the point that being oneself is a problem of liberation which takes courage and takes pains and may mean suffering. The nucleus of all problems is whether a person dares or whether this person has capitulated and to find out how he or she dares to hide this capitulation. That's what most people do: they hide the fact that he or she has capitulated and that they have given up this puzzle that they had. They permit themselves to be managed, but they find ways and means to hide from it.

Here the problem is of taking sides. There is no neutrality in this question which leads to a very interesting question— that of value judgments. Freud and perhaps many people would say that is a value judgment about these parents. Well, is it a value judgment if somebody is diagnosed as having cancer? Is it a value judgment to say he will probably die from this illness, or somebody will die from some crazy diet he is using or get sick from it? It is not a value judgment. This is a statement of facts, of cause and effects, which is as valid in psychic terms as it is in physical terms, except in physical terms you can prove it. In psychic terms you can prove it too at the end of one's life. But people naturally don't want to know that.

The question is: What can the analyst do to help this process of the revolution, of the liberation of a person? What active help can he do? How can he help and affect this process? I think that is in itself a very significant function of all education and of all therapy. I include education, although education is a different story. Usually education is a social institution and it is certainly not meant to lead people to freeing themselves and to become independent. That is not the aim of any socially-supported institution. But that's why education contributes so little to the development of a person, in general. In analysis it's a little bit different, because the analyst has the freedom to be on his own and to be relatively independent.

This is just a general problem which I only mention here because this girl (Christiane) is still at a point where she doesn't see another world, where she doesn't see anything else but that she has been defeated. What these parents mean by this crazy condition I would be interested in only out of sheer curiosity about how their minds work. How would the parents prevent that they see each other and sleep together? Would they send a detective? And how are the young people going to respect that? What was Peter's reaction when he heard this condition?

Reporter: Peter's reaction was one of a great deal of unhappiness. He continued to see her for about a month, surreptitiously meeting her in Frankfurt, and then he gave up. He said: "It's all we can do."

Fromm: When it became so explicitly and unavoidably clear how destructive the parents were, how did Christiane react to Peter's decision to drop her in order not to lose his career? Because then he could find another job somewhere else, he is just not willing to give up this top prize.

Reporter: When Peter decided to go along with the father's decision Christiane became at first very hurt. I asked her what hurt means, and she said "upset" and I asked her what upset means and it finally came out that she could be angry with him. If he were a man of greater courage, given his proven abilities, he could have done something else. But I guess though she was angry, she was disappointed but it wasn't a kind of rage at being played with or misused. She also feels that she herself was culpable.

Fromm: Of course she botched it up herself again, because if she had talked, the proper strategy would be to first win over the father, who is sensible and receptive to her, and then after winning over the father to say to him: "Now, I need your help with mother." The father might still not have done it but by confronting the two together in the cold, it is obvious how they would react. So Christiane hasn't done her best. It's the same thing again as the application for the graduate school of literature; she does not really dare to do what she wants. But she does it in an ineffective way when she is intelligent enough to know better. She knows her father quite well. Of course this does not contribute to her sense of self-esteem.

Peter is a man who has pretended to be so much in love with her and then as it is to be expected, when it is a matter of becoming president eventually, that it is even more important than even a great love. I think that most people do act this way today, statistically speaking. But it's just too bad for Christiane, that she has to experience that when that was the first relationship where she was probably as strongly interested and in love with a man as she ever was before. And naturally that experience drives her to this mood.

Question: Maybe it could have been a choice from her side knowing from the beginning that it didn't lead anywhere. In other words, something where she knew she would be defeated. Maybe she couldn't really deal with a situation where there was a future.

Fromm: No, she can't, that is all part of the same picture of disorientation, of running around like a chicken and not knowing what to do and no orientation, and doing things just as she went to the parents and told them that she got this new and better job. She calls up her mother. Well, how stupid, but it's not stupid she doesn't know any better. That is the only place in which she is somebody, otherwise it's a desert. You might say, to stay with the desert, her parents are the only oasis. And she knows if she goes out of this oasis she will die from thirst. She has no one to help her, she has no map, she has no compass, she has nothing. And that is literally so; that is how she feels. So how could she act differently, feeling this is the situation?

Question: How would you have helped her if possible to have gotten her energies, to have started rebelling?

Fromm: I would have incited her to rebellion, very strongly. In any case, I would have tried it. Of course, one never knows what happens when one incites people to rebellion. But that would be my first attempt, because I know unless she does that, she will never get well or have a happy life. She is like in a posthypnotic state where she has to fulfill what was suggested to her.

Question: Is it possible that the relationship with Peter was probably motivated by some unconscious desire to rebel against her parents?

Fromm: Yes, but these are all the same ineffective rebellions which only lead to new defeats. This is different again, you can observe them in life again and again. People want to rebel but they rebel in such a way that they are sure to be defeated. They prove to themselves in a tricky way that you see, rebellion is useless. A son, for example, makes a big scene to his father, and shouts at him and accuses him and plays crazy. The next day he comes back and apologizes—and he has to apologize because he behaved so childishly and so irrationally. If he had told his father in clear words what he really thinks, but to the point, then he would have won a victory. Because then the father would have been embarrassed. So the father is again in a superior position. That happens all the time.

Therefore I would have questioned Christiane earlier in therapy very clearly that this was another form of ineffectual rebellion before she became so involved with Peter. I might have talked about the possible strategy of this man and would have brought up that it is expected to end this way, because basically this is a man for whom career—and not just career, not to make a living—but top career, top success is more important than being as much in love as he ever would be.

I make these comments simply because I want to use the occasion of a case to express my own idea about therapy. If I look back at my own therapy, then I'm usually ashamed about the way I have analyzed people five years earlier because I have made this mistake and that mistake. It is a terribly complex process and I know very well that naturally from short notes one does not give half the story because many things are necessarily very lacking. So what I said is not mainly a reaction to the presented case but using this "text" for remarks of my thinking in analysis, about analytic therapy. I didn't really speak too much to the material, I just used the material for my own purposes of expressing certain ideas. More I didn't intend.

10

Specified Methods to Cure Modern Character Neuroses

[For modern character neuroses it is typical that people suffer on themselves. To cure these modern neuroses additional steps beyond classic psychoanalysis are necessary. The last chapter is focused on these methods.]

Changing One's Own Action

First of all I believe it is necessary to change one's action and not only to analyze and to be aware of oneself. If one is only aware of oneself without at the same time making steps which are the consequences of this new awareness, then all awareness remains ineffective. One can analyze oneself and know everything for so many years but it will not be effective if it remains sterile, if at the same time one does not accompany it by changes in one's practice of life. These changes may be small, but one cannot proceed in this way as you find it in some leftist philosophers who say: when the revolution comes, then we will have better men. Marcuse says this, but before the revolution any attempt to become a better man is only reactionary. That is of course plain nonsense in my opinion because after the revolution comes and nobody has changed, the revolution will just repeat all the misery of what has happened before. Revolution will be made by people who have no idea of what a better human life could be.

What changes what one makes in oneself is a very subtle thing. One cannot make so much, but one must also not be overcareful. It is a very important task I think in analysis to keep constantly in mind how a person stimulates himself and stimulates new discoveries by experiencing the feelings. One has to look for the experiences and particularly resistances which a person has in making the next step, in acting differently. Otherwise one remains somewhat in an unreal situation, in spite of all the subjective experiences one has. What these changes are depends entirely on the situation. Psychoanalysis has the great danger that everything is put under analysis and that people believe only when the analysis is over, is finished, then will they make the changes. I am convinced that one has to begin making changes before, and the question is only what changes and the problem of graduality, and the quality of changes one can make—changes which are not unrealistic, which don't go beyond one's capacity to make them at the moment. This, of course, is a very serious and difficult problem.

Developing Interest in the World

The second point is to stop one's over-interest in oneself. Also here psychoanalysis has a great danger. People who really are only interested in themselves find a tremendously rich field to practice narcissism. Nothing is important in the world but their problems. Look at the woman of the case history [Christiane]: What it is that interests her? Nothing really, except her suffering, her husband, her parents, and her child. But there is a woman who has studied, who is educated, who lives in a time where a wealth of human culture is open to her, books, music, art, everything. For heaven's sake, you can read all the most beautiful books which have ever been written in the world, you can listen to all the music, there is a tremendous choice, you can walk, you can even travel. And here sits a person who is not interested in anything but her problem, or his problem.

To be only interested in one's own problems is not the way of getting well or of becoming a full human being. One cannot live in a strong and joyous and independent way if one's only interest is oneself. One must stand with two feet on the ground, but the ground must not be the pin or the needle because on that only the angels can dance, according to medieval speculations. But one cannot stand. One can live with one's feet on the ground only if this ground is broad and rich and if one is related to the world around one in a productive, interested way.

"Interested" is a poor word. There is actually in English today no word to express this kind of relationship. "Interested" would be a good word, it comes from inter-esse, to be in them, to be in there, but interest today is almost the opposite of that. If somebody says "I am interested in this" he really means I am bored by it. "That's very interesting"—that's what anyone says about a book or about an idea, by "it's very interesting" he really means to say "I don't give a damn." That is a polite way of saying that. [...]

The danger must be averted with analysis or without analysis, that a person remains concentrated about his own problems and remains separated from the world, that is to say from relating himself or herself in a detached way to all that is around him or her: to people, to ideas, to nature. [...]

How does anyone enrich his life? All the misery which is experienced by many people lies to a large extent in the fact not that they are so sick but they are separated from everything that's interesting in life, that's exhilarating in life, that is beautiful in life. They sit and fret about their problems, about their sins, about their mistakes, their symptoms, God knows what, while they could sit and enjoy life in many, many ways. Usually they say: "But I'm too depressed to do it." Well, that is in a way true, but it is not the whole answer. They don't even make an attempt, or enough of an attempt to enrich their lives because they think the best way to cure oneself is the complete concentration on one's own problems. But that is *not* the best way—it's the worst way.

Concentration on one's own problems should and must go together with an increasing enlargement and intensification of one's interest in life. This interest can be art, many things, but I think it must also be ideas. I won't think that this is just an intellectual pastime, this is the one point in which I always disagreed with Alexander Sutherland Neill of Summerhill, that he put too little emphasis on the formation of the mind. I don't think much of a purely intellectual formation of the mind, but of the enrichment of the mind. The question becomes very concrete: What does anyone read? I would say one should begin reading, and reading significant books, and reading them seriously. I have the impression that the modern method of reading is one which is directed by the idea that one should not make too much of an effort, it should be easy, it should be brief, it should be immediately pleasurable.

These are, of course, all illusions. Nothing that is worthwhile can be done or learnt without any effort, and even without some sacrifice, without discipline. The whole idea of learning to play music or anything else in eight easy lessons is just to get people's money out of their pockets. It is complete nonsense, but this is the spirit which not in its crude form pervades I think the whole population, and in spite of the fact that we publish so many books, the number of books which are seriously read, which really make a dent on a person, which really make a change in his life, I think that's very rare today.

So here it's a great question of the way in which one reads, what one reads.

In connection with reading the first point of course is that a person begins to form his or her own convictions, to have values, to have directions in which he or she wants his or her life to go. If he or she doesn't do that, he or she must flounder. It seems to me that one doesn't really read anything of the traditions, because one has to discover it by oneself. I think it's a very silly and ignorant idea, because to combine the greatest minds of the world in one person and to all discover it oneself, really shows that one is not serious. That one is not after discovery of great things, of new things, and exciting things. And yet most people don't have the experience of the intense excitement which discovery, seeing something new or seeking something new, has. But if one doesn't come eventually to a concept of life, of direction, of values, of convictions, which are not put in oneself by others but which are the result of one's own experience, but also gleaning from active, productive, and critical reading of all that is to be had in the great guides of the human mind, then I don't believe one can ever come to the point of feeling secure, of feeling safe, of having one's center.

That is all today not a very fashionable idea, because people will think that's dogmatic and people make excuses they want to find it themselves and it's authoritarian. It's basically barbarous to renounce to learn from the great things that the human race has created. That's what in my opinion it is and it is stupid. But one deprives oneself in the name of independence, in the name of rejecting authority, one deprives oneself of being fed, of being influenced, of being watered, of having the sunshine, of all that the human mind needs in order to develop. One may be a vegetarian as far as food is concerned, but if one is a vegetarian as far as mental and spiritual food is concerned and refuses most of what is there, then indeed one's mind dries up very considerably.

Learning to Think Critically

Another essential point in my opinion is to learn to think critically. Critical thinking is the only weapon and defense which man has against the dangers in life. If I do not think critically then indeed I am subject to all influences, to all suggestions, to all errors, to all lies which are spread out, with which I am indoctrinated from the first day on. One cannot be free, one cannot be one's own, one cannot have one's center in oneself unless one is able to think critically and—if you like—cynically.

Critical thinking means to become aware as children can show: children are much more critical still than adults are. When a child sees that a mother has said to Mrs. X: "Oh, how wonderful to see you" and put on all this talk, and then after Mrs. X has left said to her husband: "Oh thank God that she has gone," well, the child sees this discrepancy and maybe it still dares to ask but then its critical thinking is beaten down step by step by step. Either mother tells a lie or mother is angry, or mother is sad or mother says: "You don't understand that," and so the child's critical thinking becomes slowly stifled until no more critical thoughts come.

This critical thinking is the specific human ability. To think manipulatively—that is to say, to think how do I get, what do I do to get this and that—the chimpanzees do that very well. Chimpanzees, in fact animals, have a manipulative intelligence which is excellent. Chimpanzees in experiments have solved puzzles which I couldn't solve and many other people couldn't either they're so complicated. Again I would say, from a purely, biological standpoint, the closer I am to reality the more am I capable to live my life adequately. The less close am I to reality, the more illusions I have, the less am I capable to deal with life in an adequate way.

Marx once said a word which could also be the motto of psychoanalysis: "The demand to give up the illusions about its condition is the demand to give up a condition which needs illusions" (K. Marx, MEGA I, 1, 1, pp. 607-08). That is to say by not doing away with illusions one keeps alive circumstances which are unhealthy and which can only exist and continue because one makes oneself all these illusions.

Critical thinking is not a hobby, critical thinking is a faculty. Critical thinking is not something which you apply as a philosopher and then when you are a philosopher you think critically, but when you are at home you have given up, taken off your critical thinking. Critical thinking is a quality, is a faculty, it's an approach to the world, to everything; it's by no means critical in the sense of hostile, of negativistic, of nihilistic, but on the contrary critical thought stands in the service of life, in the service of removing obstacles to life individually and socially which paralyze us.

It takes courage if one lives in a world in which critical thinking is discouraged. But one should also not overestimate the courage it takes. I am not talking here even now of critical speaking or of critically acting. Critically thinking is possible even for the man in a dictatorship. If he doesn't want to risk his life he may not talk critically, but he may think critically. Yet he will feel much much happier and freer than the man who is caught in his thoughts and who is a prisoner of a thought system which he doesn't believe himself. One could write volumes on the connection of critical thinking and mental health, and neurosis, and happiness. If philosophers in general talked more *ad personam*, that is to say more in reference to what the philosophy means in my life and in your life, then indeed critical thinking would, philosophy would, be much more obviously a field of great personal significance. Whether you deal with Socrates or Kant or Spinoza, the essential point is that they teach critical thinking.

To Know Oneself and to Get Aware of One's Unconscious

I want to mention three other points which are very important additions to the classic psychoanalytic methods for curing modern character neuroses. A first method is to know oneself and to get aware of one's unconscious. These words themselves mean absolutely nothing when they are used in a purely intellectual sense. It's so easy today: being aware of yourself, conscious, unconscious—those are now the slogans. Even the dirtiest little business proposition uses the Delphic "know thyself." So these words themselves become pure theoretical cerebral concepts.

If one really thinks about what these words mean or talks about it, all this becomes vivid. It's the same thing actually as when you see a painting. If you look at a painting of Rembrandt—I mention him because he's one of my favorite painters—you can see that same painting a hundred times and it's always new, it's always fresh, it brings you to life and you bring the painting to life for yourself. But you can pass by and remark: "Ah, Rembrandt, *The Man with the Helmet*" and then walk to the next painting. You have seen it, all right, but you never saw it.

The same holds true with personal relationships. Who sees another person really? Hardly anybody. We are all satisfied and happy to see and to show only our surfaces. That's why our contacts are poor, just poor, or hardly exist against this poverty of contact, it is covered up by a kind of camaraderie and friendliness and smiling, smiling, smiling.

The next question is: What does it mean to know oneself? To know oneself is not only to be aware of what we do but to become aware of what is unconscious to us, of what we don't know. This is in a way the great discovery of Freud to have demonstrated this and to have made it very explicit, more explicit perhaps than it has ever been made, and to enlarge thereby the field of knowing oneself considerably. "Knowing oneself" a hundred years ago meant essentially to know everything we know about ourselves. Today it means to know ourselves inasmuch as we are aware of ourselves and inasmuch as we are unaware of ourselves; that is to say, to bring to the light the largest sector of our own psychic life—namely that sector which operates separated from our normal conscious thinking, that sector that comes on to the stage at night when we dream, or in psychosis when we hallucinate.

You might also describe it in a different way. To know oneself in this new dimension, in this third dimension of one's unconscious life, means to be free, means to wake up. The fact is that most of us are half asleep while we believe ourselves to be awake. We are actually only awake enough to perform the tasks which are necessary to make a living; for that we are awake enough and some people are damned awake about that. But for the task of being ourself, for the task that transcends that animal function, of feeling ourselves, for the task which goes beyond doing—being a feeding machine and a love machine—for this task we need other insight, rather than the one which we have enough of in the state of the half-awakeness. If you consider that the Buddha means "the awakened one," then you have a symbolic expression of what I am trying to say. The person who is truly aware of him- or herself, who penetrates through the surface to the roots of his existence, he or she is awakened.

It is peculiar, looking at the life of most people, how half-asleep they are. Nobody knows from nothing, nobody knows what he wants to do, what the consequences are. People, inasmuch as they deal with problems of their human existence, are ignorant. When they deal with business, they know very well. Then they know how one gets ahead, how one manipulates other people and oneself. But when it comes to the question of living they are half awake or less than half awake.

I should like to transmit the impression on being awakened which I have on the basis of my own experience, and which I should like the interested to have about oneself or about other people. It takes time. To be aware of this state of half awakeness, when people believe themselves to be so wide awake. In fact the paradox is that we are more awake when we are asleep, to ourselves, than we are when we are awake. When we are asleep or when we are crazy, at least in certain stages of craziness, then indeed we are terribly aware of ourselves as subjects, as feeling persons, as people; only that this awareness remains separate from the external life. It exists only as long as it is dark or, biologically speaking, as long as the organism is freed from the function of manipulating the world, defending itself, or going about seeking food.

But as soon as we wake up we go to sleep. Then we lose all insight, all awakeness for the more subtle processes of our feeling, of our knowledge, and we are asleep to all, and that's the way we live. Is it a wonder that people make so little sense of their lives? That people are so unhappy in the midst of plenty? That people who have everything that would be necessary to make out of life the very best life can give, flounder, are unhappy, dissatisfied, disappointed, and at the end of life have often a very bitter and sad feeling that they have lived and yet they have never been alive. That they were awake but they never woke up? That is what it means to be aware of oneself.

To become aware of his unconscious one doesn't need to be analyzed. It needs only a certain interest and a certain courage to really experience. One, for instance, must have the courage to experience: "For so many years I believed I liked this man and believed that this is a decent man and suddenly I see it is not true at all. I never liked him, I always knew that he is not a decent man."

Strangely enough, we also know what we repress. There is really no word for this knowledge which we have, for this awareness which we have of things which we have repressed. It's not "preconscious" in Freud's sense, of course, because preconscious is something which is close to consciousness. But it is not repressed in the sense, either, that it is completely separated from our system. It is of course protected very often through what one calls resistance, but strangely enough you also very often find if a person is analyzed and the analyst may tell him something, or also without analysis that a person may see something, have an insight and suddenly know: "But I knew that all the time, I knew that all my life. It is not really new. I knew it and at the same time I didn't know it."

There is this phenomenon of awareness which is neither conscious nor is it entirely unconscious in the sense of the classical repressed state. This phenomenon has even certain consequences for psychoanalytic technique. One speaks so much of the resistance of a patient. That is perfectly justified and the resistance, as a protection against something which we are afraid of being aware of, is very strong. But very often, if the analyst for instance tells the patient something he sees, straight: "This is what I see, I cannot prove it to you but this is what I hear," then it will not so rarely happen that the patient says: "Oh, you are right, I never knew that, but I did know it, too." When this sensing is expressed by somebody else strongly, clearly, and truthfully enough and in no fantastic and hypertheoretical terms, the person may say: "Oh Lord, yes, that's me, that's right, that's true."

How often that happens depends on the depth of the resistance. If the resistance is massive, that will not help. In those cases, however, where the resistance is not massive but where the fortress is only lightly defended, something which is unconscious, the awareness of it, the sensing of it, may come up immediately, while it might take a much longer time to go over that resistance if the analyst cannot state first directly: "Now, look here, this is what I see." It is a matter of the skill of the analyst to know when he can do that, or when he can't. In some cases it doesn't make any difference because if the resistance is that great the patient will answer: "Well, that's clear enough what you are saying," and that's that. In some cases it can be dangerous because in spite of the fact that patient says: "No, that's all nonsense, here," in his unconscious there is something which reacts to it which does not simply react like "This is nonsense," and the next day or an hour later this person has a severe depression, because he could not stand this sudden truth. Now, if this whole thing is so repressed, why does he react that way? Something in him has heard it.

It is too convenient for us personally always to think: "If I am not aware of it, it's repressed, and if it's repressed, maybe I have to go to a psychoanalyst for a year, and if I can't do that or don't want to do it, leave it alone." But it's not that simple. If I really train myself to be sensitive to it, I might discover something about which, without even the help of an analyst, I find out one day: "Oh, that isn't quite as I think."

The sensitivity necessary to get aware of one's own unconscious is known to us: If we for instance drive a car, we are terribly sensitive to the noise of the car without thinking about it. We notice the finest noise, the slightest difference. We can think of something entirely different, be completely concentrated on the view in front of us—but if there is the slightest change in the noise level, or in the quality of the tone, we are immediately aware of it.

Becoming Aware of One's Body

Another method for curing modern character neuroses is the awareness of one's body. By that I mean something which is sometimes called sensitivity. I refer to the bodily awareness which most people do not have because they feel the body only when they have a pain. But we don't feel our body when we have no pain. Very few people do. To become aware of one's body, not only of one's breathing, but of one's whole body, one's posture, when one is cramped—this is a very important addition to becoming aware of one's mind. I do recommend it to anybody as a very important adjunct to the analysis of one's mind which goes on in analysis.

The awareness of one's body, and the reconstruction of one's bodily experience, and a greater awareness by arriving at a much greater harmony and uncramping of the body, is of great importance. I have taken for years the Elsa Gindler method and now for quite a few years learning the T'ai Chi which is a very exacting and very relaxing set of Chinese movements, and I have greatly benefited from it. In certain instances certain types of massage as Georg Groddek and Wilhelm Reich had found them, can have a very good effect.

If a person really learns how to free himself from the inside he will know that also in his bodily posture. One sees the difference between a repressed, inwardly cramped person and the person after he has loosened up, has lost a great deal of his repressions. One can watch it in his bodily posture, in his gestures, even though he has not particularly trained himself in the method of body sensitivity. It's not only that the body, the awareness has an effect on one's inner decramping, on one's inner confidence, but it works both ways. To the same extent one gets freer inwardly, one will also be freer physically, in one's body.

It is very important not to forget that body relaxation alone is not enough. I have known quite a few people who really had achieved very much in terms of a complete harmony of their bodily posture—or what looks like a complete harmony—but who have solved less of their deep reaching problems, of their identity, of their sense of self, of their closeness, of the depth and reality of their relationships to people. So I would still give the primary importance to the experience of oneself in the analytic sense, and this is greatly helped by any method which at the same time does this with the body, leads to greater harmony and relaxing of the body.

I can measure my inner state of mind by observing my posture. It changes accordingly: if I feel less well my posture will be one of tiredness, of slouching, and if I feel well, inwardly well, then my posture will be different (and I am in no way a good example to others of what the posture should be). The body is of course an expression of everything that goes in: that refers to gesture, it refers to the way one sits, and it refers to the way one walks. One can recognize a person looking to his back; many people can more easily identify it by the way he walks than one might by his face, because a walk is the least intended and the least conscious move, and therefore the most honest one. The same holds true for gestures. Of course there are people who have learned gestures like a ham actor, but anyone who has some sense knows the difference between what's false, what's learnt.

The same holds true for handwriting, incidentally. You have indeed sometimes handwritings which are just beautiful; the handwriting is so beautiful, so artistic, so impressive, you say: "What a beautiful handwriting." But very often a good graphologist will tell you that this handwriting is completely planned, that is to say the person has learned to write in such a way that gives him the air, which makes the impression of being a very artistic, highly developed, and a wonderful person. One can do that. And it's not even necessarily that one does that intentionally, that one has a plan to do it. But one catches on to the trick. A good graphologist notices the difference between what is directed in that kind of handwriting and what is genuine. Sometimes you can see it without being a graphologist—that people who write in a specific way that they usually think is beautiful, but when they are in a hurry, they suddenly write something and you see: "For heaven's sake, that's an entirely different handwriting," because at that moment they don't have time to paint their calligraphy.

Every bodily expression, even the most subtle one, is an immediate expression of our souls. Dr. Rothschild, one of the most gifted psychiatrists, living as a psychoanalyst now in Jerusalem, could give you when he was much younger an analysis of the character of a person by looking at the soles of his shoes. He could reconstruct very intuitively from the way the soles are worn to the way you walk and he didn't even have to observe the person walking. From the way his soles were worn he could see how the person walked and from there he could deduct who the person was. Independently from being gifted in this way we all should develop a sense of understanding the meaning of a gesture, the meaning of a posture, the meaning of a walk. Then one can go to a more difficult problem, the meaning of the whole body, the physical beat of a person, in terms of who this person is. It is not only that our functional things are expressive of our inner life, but also that to an extent the way we are built is also symbolic of something we are. But that is a very difficult problem. It's a problem that is still very little explored, although for instance in the typology of Kretschmer and of Sheldon there is shown very clearly the connection between physical build and, for instance, manic depressive or schizoid traits.

To Concentrate and Meditate

Other methods are concentration and meditation exercises, things which are done regularly and with great discipline. One has to interrupt a life in which one is constantly affected by thousands and thousands of impressions and stimuli, and one has to experience being with oneself quietly and in stillness. Concentration exists very little in modern times. People are distracted. So you listen to the radio and at the same time you talk and you do three things at the same time. Even if you listen to a conversation, it often lacks this one quality of concentration.

To learn concentration, to be concentrated on everything one does, is of course a condition for any kind of achievement, in any field. Without any question it can be said that any achievement, whether that is to be a good carpenter, or to be a good cook, or to be a good philosopher, or to be a good physician, or to be just very alive, depends entirely on the capacity to be really concentrated. "Really concentrated" means that at that moment there is nothing else in your mind but that which you are doing and that you almost forget everything else. That's also the essence of a conversation of anything worthwhile to talk about to another person. At that moment the two people who talk are concentrated on what they are talking about, and on each other.

Nature has in a way given an example, because the sexual act is impossible without the minimum of concentration. If people thought of other things and of the stock market, they just wouldn't succeed in sexual intercourse because it's by the nature of the thing that there is a certain amount of concentration necessary even to function. But that is only so to speak a hint nature has given us. But most people don't take that hint. In their relationships they are not concentrated.

Take for instance a simple thing: the American habit of not inviting one person or two persons, but inviting at least four or six. They do so because they are afraid of being alone with two others, afraid of the closeness or of the possible concentration that would require. But if there are six people there is no concentration really, one talks about this—and it's like a big three-ring circus. If you are ten, then of course it's completely without any concentration. While if two people talk together—even if they talk very little or even if they talk about something very simple, if this is a real communication at this very moment—there is nothing more important than that one talks to the other. To the degree to which that is not there, nothing really happens.

To start with concentration exercises the simplest thing is just to sit and to close the eyes and to try not to think of anything but just to feel your own breathing. Once you think about your breathing you don't feel it; that is to say, your body is not aware of your breathing. Once you begin to think, you are not aware of your breathing anymore, because then you think about your breathing. That holds true for practically all experiences. Once you think about them, you stop experiencing.

To give a simple example to illustrate the difference between thinking and experiencing: A dancer remembers a dance movement, but he doesn't remember it in his head. A dancer's body remembers it, her memory is in her body. Of course the memory is still up in the brain, but it is not that she thinks what comes next; in fact in a complicated dance if she would start to think what comes next she is lost. Her or his body is aware of movement and has an excellent memory. The same thing holds true for a musical score, you don't think what comes, you hear it; your memory is here, but it's not in the thought. It's obvious really what it means to experience, but as often people forget the most obvious thing.

When you try to sit and not to think of anything, then you will find that's rather difficult, very difficult. You will find that many things come to your mind. You think of books, of everything. That means you are not concentrating, because you are attracted or distracted by many things. You can then see what thoughts come to your mind and what's really on your mind. That's a nice piece of self-analysis. Then you think of your job, or this and that and what you are doing. You will find that those things come in your mind which are important for you in some way, not directly often, but indirectly.

You must really analyze whatever comes to your mind. It's a matter of practice to learn to be concentrated. You sit and you—let us say—look at these flowers. You sit there for five minutes, ten minutes, and you do nothing but look at these flowers. When thoughts come, you don't get excited and discouraged and say: "Oh Lord, I can't do it," but you say: "All right, naturally they come." When you have done that for a week, four weeks, four years, then you will have learned to concentrate.

To learn the practice of concentration I would like to recommend to you a book which I think is very useful: *The*

Heart of Buddhist Meditation is about Buddhist awareness, Buddhist meditation, and is written by a Nyanaponika Mahathera, whom I know quite well. He is a Buddhist monk who is by origin German. He lives in Sri Lanka and is a very learned man, combining Buddhism with the German scholarly tradition. He has translated many texts from Pali and Sanskrit. Nyanaponika is also a very interesting person who has achieved a great deal in his own life. He is very alive, extremely stimulating, and there is never a moment which could he in the remotest sense be called dead. His *The Heart of Buddhist Meditation* is an excellent description on hand of the Buddhist texts, of what Buddhist meditation is centered around: mindfulness. Mindfulness means awareness: I am fully aware at every moment of my body, including my posture, anything that goes on in my body, and I am fully aware of my thoughts, of what I think; I am fully concentrated—is precisely this full awareness.

To Discover One's Own Narcissism

Freud's discovery of the concept of narcissism has been one of his greatest discoveries, although Freud, by explaining the concept in terms of his own frame of reference of libido theory, has narrowed it down. According to Freud one has to speak of primary narcissism where all the libido is still within the Ego and later in the Id, then the narcissism is sent out to object. If the narcissism is then taken back again to the Ego or the Id, you speak of secondary narcissism. This view of Freud is a very mechanistic concept, as the whole libido theory is. If one liberates the concept of narcissism like some other concepts of Freud from the libido concept, and if one uses libido as Jung in fact has done in a much broader sense of psychic energy, then it will turn out that the concept of narcissism is about one of the most important concepts Freud ever discovered.

According to my understanding, the narcissistic person is a

person for whom reality is only that which goes on subjectively. His own thoughts, his own feelings, and so on are real; they represent reality. Therefore the little infant is extremely narcissistic because originally there is not yet a reality outside. The psychotic patient is extremely narcissistic because his only reality is constituted by his own inner experiences. And most of us are more or less narcissistic, that is to say more or less drawn to take for real only that which is within ourselves, and not that which refers to another person. I think for the understanding of man, that is to say for the understanding of ourselves, the understanding of narcissism is one of the most important things, and it has not found the attention really, even in orthodox analysis.

I must describe here a little bit more clearly what this narcissism is in terms of our experience. Let us say you have written a journal paper or you are just writing it and you read your first draft of two pages. You think that's wonderful, it's crazy. You show it to your friend and you are deeply hurt when the friend doesn't think this is the greatest thing of the century. You read it the next day again and you think, "What, this doesn't make any sense, it's nothing, it's badly organized, not clear." The explanation is it's plainly because while you were writing you were in a narcissistic mood. A narcissistic mood means here that everything that pertains to me—my thought, my feelings, my body, my interests—all that is real, and the rest of the world which is not related to me is not real, has no color, is gray, has no weight. I measure with two completely different measurements: That which is mine, returns to me, is my opinion, that is written in big letters, that's color, that's alive. I feel because I say that makes it true, I don't have to have the proof. I am enamored of myself, which means to say with my work, with my thoughts. But what is outside, that doesn't make any impression, that I hardly feel.

The following example is quite frequent and is, at the same time, a good illustration of other aspects of narcissism. Take for instance a man who is married and needs to have many love affairs. He expects his wife to be delighted when he comes and tells her all the wonderful conquests he makes. He comes to the analyst and says: "You see, she doesn't love me, because instead of being happy about my conquests and being interested in what I am doing and how many girls fall for me, she shows no interest in it." The absurd arguments of this man show that he is only capable of experiencing him, what pertains to him; that is to say *he* is very happy because he needs that kind of thing, but he is perfectly incapable of seeing the reality of his wife, namely that she quite naturally is not very happy about it. If she were sitting there and would listen to his stories and be very delighted about them, then she would be neurotic because she would act like a mother and look upon the man like a little boy who tells his adventures, how many games he won in football.

A narcissistic person lives on the feeding of his narcissism. The narcissistic person is a terribly insecure person because all his feelings are not based, none of these things are based on reality. He makes a statement but this statement is not achieved after having thought, by thoughtfulness, by work, by being in touch with the material, but simply because he makes it. It is his statement and because it is *his* statement it is true. But he is in great need to have his narcissism confirmed because when it is not confirmed then he begins to doubt everything. Then who is he? If the statement of a narcissistic person is true because it is his or her statement, he or she cannot fall back and say: "Well, I'll do better next time." To give an example: A person said something at a party, he may be very intelligent, he has always been admired. Then he said something which was a little stupid, or he made a mistake and people found out. Maybe it's not that bad, but he will fall into a deep depression. His armor was pierced, because he loses faith in the wonderfulness of everything he is doing. Since his whole existence, his whole security, is only rooted in the conviction of his, this subjective conviction, if he meets with somebody who criticizes him or views him with disappointment, he feels he is attacked. Then his whole system of self-belief, of self-inflation, is pierced and he will get very depressed or very furious.

There is no greater fury than to hurt the narcissism of a narcissistic person. He will forgive everything else but never to hurt his narcissism, and that is indeed something which one should always remember. You can do almost anything to a narcissistic person, but if you pierce his narcissism or hurt his narcissism there will be a rage whether he shows it or not, and there will be a sense of revenge because it's almost like killing him.

People who are very narcissistic are often very attractive because he or she is so sure of himself or herself. They ooze self-confidence. He is attractive, and let us say the girl falls in love with him and she admires him because he is so sure of himself—nobody is as sure of himself as he is. If a person is not so narcissistic he cannot be sure of himself, of anything. After a few months she thinks he is wrong in something and she criticizes him. At this point this is the whole reason why he loved her: that she admired him more than the other girls. That's usually the choice, there is the competition of admiration, so she admired him most and now she undermines the whole situation by criticizing him. To him that means: "She doesn't believe in me, she is a danger, she is a threat." He will do any kind of reaction: He can either be so nasty that she doesn't dare to do it again, or he can leave her, and the usual complaint is that she doesn't understand him. His complaint that he or she doesn't understand the other is the standard complaint, especially for narcissists, because they think they're not understood.

Narcissistic people can also live a *folie à deux*. I remember a case of a mother and her daughter who were both convinced, and said so, that they were the only people who were clean, decent, and knew how to cook, in the whole country. Anybody will say that's crazy, because this completely uncritical belief in their greatness and infallibility is a manifestation of sheer narcissism. When a man says: "My country is the most wonderful country, we are better than anyone else," then you can say he is patriotic, loyal, a good citizen, and nobody says he is crazy because it is shared by everybody else. Everybody else likes to feel that too, and people of another country like to feel that about their country. When the two get together there is a tremendous hate, because each has to preserve the collective narcissism in which he shares with others in the wonderful feeling of his greatness.

The collective narcissism is the narcissism of the poor man. The rich man, the powerful man, has enough reality to back up his narcissism by his money, by his power, by those elements of reality which give him the feeling of his power. The poor man—and I don't just mean the poor man but the average man, what does he have? He is employed somewhere, he has nothing to say, he is afraid of his competitors, his whole life is a rat race—so whom can he impress? His little boy and his dog perhaps, but the boy grows older too and his wife has also learned to take care of herself. But when he can participate in collective narcissism, when he can feel as a member of this nation, I am the greatest—I am more wonderful than anybody else. So he can indulge in this narcissistic experience, but since it is extended to the group there is consensus between all members of this group. In fact it unites these people and strengthens them when they can commonly express their faith in their extraordinary qualities. That is what they call nationalism, that is at the bottom of most wars.

A tremendous amount of collective narcissism one can find in family narcissism. There is a secret narcissism of families. Think of all these families where the mother comes from a little higher life, a step up the social ladder, and will feel forever that her family is better than that of the husband or vice versa, and the child already from the beginning hears how wonderful the Cohens or the Smiths are and how lacking the other side is. And then it's their class, because the family carries with it at the same time a tremendous class narcissism. You don't just marry somebody from another class, rationalized by people from the same background who understand each other better. But the proof is that they don't, because the same background affords lack of initiative, lack of pleasure, makes them doubly unhappy.

The degree of narcissism of people nevertheless varies a great deal. You find extremely narcissistic people short of being crazy, short of being insane. The psychotic person is very withdrawn because he has been so badly hurt by the world, he has been so anxious to renew contact that he withdraws. But he is also much more sensitive towards men than is a non-psychotic narcissistic person, who often is very insensitive because he is not capable of seeing, of knowing, of considering what goes on in another person.

The very narcissistic person is so certain because he is not concerned with how things are. He can speak with a certainty because all his certainty depends on the fact of what he thinks, and if that's what he thinks, it is true. To give an example for a paranoid phenomenon: Let us say a person thinks of another one who is his enemy, or he dislikes him. This may be perfectly true. He may sometimes even be a little afraid the man may do him some harm. What is the paranoid person's reaction? He is convinced the man is planning to murder him, and this conviction is unshakable because he has converted his subjective experience of feeling the other's hostility, which to him is a fact. That is a fact, and therefore he believes in the fact because his subjective feelings of the other's hostility are as good as a fact, and reality does not enter into that picture.

The same holds true with a delusion. When a person sees— let us say—his mother has become a lion. This is often a topic of dreams of men. Now, in a dream that's normal, although a dream, as Freud has said, is a transitory psychosis in which we do not see reality as it is; our own subjective experience makes reality. But when a person says, full of fright and terror: "My mother is a lion, she'll eat me," and he sees the lion enter and he says: "There is a lion coming," and thinks that is real, then we say he is crazy, he is insane. He has a delusion, namely that his mother is a lion, when actually all he has in reality is a great fright of her. But because his subjective fright is the same as reality, because his feelings make reality, then he can say, he can see in her, that she is a lion, and his whole sensory apparatus and what we call his sense of reality has completely disappeared.

To understand narcissism is one of the keys to the understanding of irrational actions of people, and to understand oneself; one's irrational reactions are to a large extent based on narcissistic phenomena. To analyze a very narcissistic person is extremely difficult because he is relatively unapproachable. And he will usually react by saying the analyst is dumb, hostile, envious, stupid, anything in order to escape from the feeling that his grandeur is not preserved, because it's a vital matter for him to keep up his image. So it's a matter which can be done only very carefully, very slowly.

The degree of narcissism of people varies a great deal. You find extremely narcissistic people short of being crazy, short of being insane. And yet you find among those who are not insane, aside from the extremely narcissistic people, people whose narcissism is not much less than that and each one can by self-observation, by comparison, and by observation of others find out about his narcissism. It is impossible to talk about narcissism theoretically without having experienced in oneself one's narcissism, or having clearly seen it in another person, but in a way so that one can really see it and not just label it. Without that experience it just doesn't make sense to talk about it because one talks about the other side of the moon.

Narcissism is a crucial problem of human development. You could summarize all teachings, whether it's Buddhist, prophetic Jewish, Christian, or you can take then a humanist statement— you can say essentially what all of them are saying to overcome your narcissism. That is the beginning of all love, of all brotherliness, because in this narcissism people are estranged from each other. Narcissism is confused with self-love.[1] In the philosophic tradition you find it very clear that narcissism or egocentricity is something entirely different from self-love. Because self-love is love, and in love it doesn't make any difference who the object of my love is. I am a human being myself.

Man must have an affirmative, loving attitude towards oneself. The egocentric person in reality is a person who does not love himself, and so he is greedy. In general a greedy person is a person who is not satisfied. Greediness is always the result of deep frustration. The satisfied person is not greedy, about power or food or anything else. Greed is always the result of an emptiness inside. That is why you find people, for instance, who are very anxious or depressed start to eat compulsively, obsessionally, because they have a feeling of emptiness.

Each individual if he wants really to develop and to grow, one of his main attempts should be to recognize his narcissism. One has to try it. You recognize it slowly, and slowly you make already a good step, you make a step forward, and if your recognition increases, it's best. But it's terribly difficult to recognize it because you are your own judge, that is to say you believe in what you think, but who is to correct you? Who is to show you that you are wrong? From your standpoint you don't feel it, you have no point of orientation.

It is the same thing with a dancer who makes exercises. An important point for dancers is that very often they do not know subjectively how good their exercise was. That's why they have to look in the mirror, because from pure subjective feeling the dancer does not know whether he made a beautiful movement, whether the timing was right, or whether it was quick. Subjectively he doesn't know how to measure. It is like with our sense of speed; if we don't have any other point of orientation we just don't know how fast we are going. Now in narcissism another

---

[1] I have written a whole chapter about this confusion in *Man for Himself*, 1947a, pp. 119-141.

person can be the point of orientation, to tell him or her something, and he or she says: "Now look here, that's sheer nonsense," and you believe that only because you had this idea or because it's your interest. People usually don't do that, but an analyst can do that provided he has sufficient experience of his own narcissism. It's a life work to overcome one's narcissism. You might say if someone overcomes it completely he is what the Christians call a saint and what the Buddhists would call an enlightened man. Or that Eckhart calls a just man. But it doesn't matter so much how far anybody goes —what matters is in what direction he is going.

Analyzing Oneself

Finally, I would like to mention self-analysis. Analysis is successfully ended when a person begins to analyze himself every day for the rest of his life. In this sense self-analysis is the constant active awareness of oneself throughout one's life, to be aware, to increase the awareness of oneself, of one's unconscious motivations, of everything which is significant in one's mind, of one's aims, of one's contradictions, discrepancies. I can only say personally that I analyze myself every morning—combined with concentration and meditation exercises—for an hour and a half, and I wouldn't want to live without it. I consider this one of the most important things I am doing. But it cannot be done without great seriousness and without giving it the importance which it has.

Self-analysis cannot be done as a hobby once in a while or when one is in the mood. All the things which one does when one is in the mood are no good, really. Nobody becomes a good pianist when he practices scales when he is in the mood. One is never in the mood to practice scales and most musicians are never in the mood to practice scales; they do it because they have to. They know they will never play Bach if they don't practice scales. And there are many things in life, if one really wants to take life seriously, which one has to do not because they are in themselves pleasureful but because they are necessary for other things.

I don't mean to apply this to self-analysis and concentration and meditation; this is not practicing scales. On the contrary, this is an exceedingly pleasureful activity in a deeper sense of the word. It's a very satisfactory activity. It has to be learned, it has to be practiced, and if one hasn't been analyzed it is more difficult. I believe it can be done also if one hasn't been analyzed. But if one suffers from more severe difficulties, then it's very difficult, almost impossible, because one is too much caught up in one's own problems, the resistances are too great. The point is if one wants to analyze oneself, the basic resistances must have been worn down. That is to say if there are things in my life against the awareness of which there is a massive resistance, then of course I cannot analyze myself because I will persuade myself with rationalizations and so on that this is not so. So it's essentially a question of the depth or intensity of resistance. And it's a question of many other factors, which make this possible. For instance, the situation in which one lives, the strength of desire to really have a happier life.

To practice self-analysis is easier if one has been analyzed. However, if the analysis has not centered around only one's childhood problems but has taken one's whole life in terms of one's whole existence: where one is in life, what are really the consequences of what one is doing, what basic aims one has—which are usually unconscious—what real goals one has, or the lack of real goals. If you have this kind of analysis, it is much easier. Karen Horney's book about self-analysis is interesting, but I don't think it's too helpful, or helpful enough, because she does self-analysis on the basis of her own analytic knowledge.

Self-analysis must really be simple, and it can be simple. You devote every day half an hour; you can walk, brood in walking and think, for instance: "I was tired yesterday. I had enough sleep, so why was I tired?" And then you might discover: "I was really anxious." Then you might go on and ask yourself: "Why was I anxious?" And you might find that you really were angry. Or you have a headache and you might ask yourself—with a headache you might always ask yourself—"At whom am I angry?" And the headache usually disappears if you find out. A few headaches don't because they have organic reasons. Migraine, for instance, is notoriously a matter of repressed anger, constant repressed anger and reproach, and at the same time causing tension to oneself. Many psychosomatic illnesses have that function.

To analyze yourself you shouldn't try to ask yourself general questions like: "What happened in my childhood." Things will occur to you once you begin to ask yourself simple questions, trying to find out what you really feel. For instance you met a person and you might ask yourself: "What did I really feel?" Consciously you would say you like that person, but you may have in the back of your mind a little doubt, and self-analysis means you take your time, are relaxed, and begin to feel. This is also not a matter of thinking, but of experimenting with your feelings: "What do I really feel?" And you might find out that you dislike this person very much or that you are afraid of this person. Or that you didn't give a damn, that you were nice, and smiled, and liked him because this person is supposed to be important or impressed you by his title or something, or because he is the brother of your mother or something, whatever the reasons are. I would say, whoever tries to begin very simply, not with great projects, not with great theories, but very directly and simply to devote every day half an hour to just trying to feel, to sense what went on in him or her yesterday—then you will slowly learn to discover lots of things.

Most people say they have no time for that. There the thing already ends because, provided this is very important, then naturally one can make time for it. When one says: "I have no time" for something, that is already a decision. It's an excuse for a decision, meaning it's not that important. If you have to earn money you don't say: "I have no time to go to the job," because you know you will be fired and you will have nothing to eat unless your parents rescue you. But if there are no parents, nobody will rescue you. If you try self-analysis, practice it and have patience, you will see some things will happen and you will also become more independent and more free, because you don't spill out everything to somebody else. One has a certain capacity to contain things in oneself, instead of constantly leaking.

To write a diary in connection with self-analysis makes self-analysis a little unalive. Of course if one goes over it every day, then it might be helpful. I think a good thing is to write down one's dreams and to see what they really are. There should be psychoanalysts who make it a practice of just being dream interpreters rather than to treat people analytically. A person should be able to write down his or her dreams for a period, and I would greatly recommend to analysts to make it a practice that such a person can come once every four weeks with his or her dreams and ask the analyst to help in interpreting these dreams. This the analyst could offer after two or three initial hours so that the analyst knows who he is talking about and what their situation is, but then to have the role simply as a dream interpreter. I think that would be a very good method, because many people who do not need more intensive help could be helped there very greatly in their own self-development by analyzing their own dreams. There's a great advantage also that the person does not become dependent on the analyst, but he or she remains all by himself or herself.

11

Psychoanalytic "Technique"—or, the Art of Listening

While technique refers to the application of the rules of an art to its object, its meaning has undergone a subtle but important change. The technical has been applied to the rules referring to the mechanical, to that which is not alive, while the proper word for dealing with that which is alive is "art." For this reason, the concept psychoanalytic "technique" suffers from a defect because it seems to refer to a non-alive object and hence not be applicable to man.

We are on safe ground to say that psychoanalysis is a process of understanding man's mind, particularly that part which is not conscious. It is an *art* like the understanding of poetry.

Like all art it has its own *rules and norms*:

- The basic rule for practicing this art is the complete concentration of the listener.
- Nothing of importance must be on his mind, he must be optimally free from anxiety as well as from greed.
- He must possess a freely-working imagination which is sufficiently concrete to be expressed in words.
- He must be endowed with a capacity for empathy with

another person and strong enough to feel the experience of the other as if it were his own.

- The condition for such empathy is a crucial facet of the capacity for love. To understand another means to love him—not in the erotic sense, but in the sense of reaching out to him and of overcoming the fear of losing oneself.
- Understanding and loving are inseparable. If they are separate, it is a cerebral process and the door to essential understanding remains closed.

The *goal* of the therapeutic process is to understand the unconscious (repressed) affects and thoughts, and to make aware and to understand their roots and functions.

The *basic rule* is to instruct the patient to say everything as far as he can and that he should mention if he leaves out something. There is a special emphasis that for the patient there is no moral obligation of any kind, not even to say the truth. (The analyst should eventually notice if the patient lies, because if he doesn't he lacks competence.)

The analyst should answer all *questions* about himself which are on public record and which the patient has a right to know—such as age, training, social origin. In others the patient would have to show why he has a legitimate interest or whether he wants to reverse the situation and analyze the psychoanalyst (because of resistance, for instance).

The therapeutic relationship shall not be characterized by an atmosphere of polite conversation and of small talk, but by directness. No lie must be expressed by the psychoanalyst. The analyst must not try to please, nor impress, but rest within himself or herself. That means he or she must have worked on himself or herself.

Bibliography

Akeret, R. U. "Reminiscences of Supervision with Erich Fromm," in *Contemporary Psychoanalysis*, New York: Academic Press, Vol. 11 (1975), pp. 461–463.

Bacciagaluppi, M. (1989) "Erich Fromm's Views on Psychoanalytic 'Technique,'" in *Contemporary Psychoanalysis*, New York: Academic Press, Vol. 25 (No. 2, April 1989), pp. 226–243.

——.1991: "More Frommian themes: core-to-core relatedness and 'there is nothing human which is alien to me.'" Paper presented at a Workshop on Frommian Therapeutic Practice, August 30–September 1, 1991, in Verbania-Pallanza, unpublished typescript, p. 11.

——.1991a: "The Clinical Fromm: Patient's Change. Introduction," in *Contemporary Psychoanalysis*, New York: William Alanson White Institute, Vol. 27 (No. 4, October 1991), p. 579f.

——.1993: "Ferenczi's Influence on Fromm," in L. Aron and A. Harris, eds., *The Legacy of Sándor Ferenczi*, Hillsdale and London: Analytic Press, 1993, pp. 185–198.

——.1993a: "Fromm's Views on Narcissism and the Self," in J. Fiscalini and A. L. Grey, eds., *Narcissism and the Interpersonal Self*, New York: Columbia University Press, 1993, p. 91–106.

Bacciagaluppi, M., and Biancoli, R. "Frommian Themes in a Case of Narcissistic Personality Disorder," in *Contemporary Psychoanalysis*, New York: William Alanson White Psychoanalytic Society, Vol. 29 (1993), pp. 441–452.

Biancoli, R. (1987) "Erich Fromms therapeutische AnnÑherung oder die Kunst der Psychotherapie," in L. von Werder, ed., *Der unbekannte Fromm: Biographische Studien* (Forschungen zu Erich Fromm, Vol. 2), Frankfurt: Haag + Herchen, 1987, pp. 101–146.

——.1992: "Radical Humanism in Psychoanalysis," in *Contemporary Psychoanalysis*, New York: William Alanson White Psychoanalytic Society, Vol. 28 (1992), pp. 695–731.

Burston, D. *The Legacy of Erich Fromm*, Cambridge (Mass.) and London: Harvard University Press, 1991.

Chrzanowski, G. (1977) "Erich Fromm," in G. Chrzanowski, "Das psychoanalytische Werk von Karen Horney, Harry Stack Sullivan und Erich Fromm,"in *Kindlers "Psychologie des 20. Jahrhunderts." Tiefenpsychologie*, Vol. 3: Die Nachfolger Freuds, ed. by von D. Eicke, Zürich: Kindler Verlag, 1977/Weinheim: Beltz Verlag, 1982, pp. 368–376; engl.: "The Work of Erich Fromm. Summing and Evaluation," in *Contemporary Psychoanalysis*, New York: Academic Press, Vol. 17 (1981), pp. 457–467.

——.1993: "Erich Fromm (1900–1980) Revisited." Reviews of E. Fromm, *The Art of Being* and *The Revision of Psychoanalysis*, in *Contemporary Psychoanalysis*, New York: William Alanson White Psychoanalytic Society, Vol. 29 (1993), pp. 541–547.

Cortina, M. "Erich Fromm's Contribution to Relational Perspectives in Psychoanalysis," typescript 1992, p. 24.

Crowley, R. M. "Tribute on Erich Fromm," in *Contemporary Psychoanalysis*, New York: Academic Press, Vol. 17 (1981), pp. 441–445.

Elkin, D. "Erich Fromm," in *Contemporary Psychoanalysis*, New York: Academic Press, Vol. 17 (1981), pp. 430–434.

Epstein, L. "Reminiscences of Supervision with Erich Fromm," in *Contemporary Psychoanalysis*, New York: Academic Press, Vol. 11 (1975), pp. 457–461.

Feiner, A. H. "Reminiscences of Supervision with Erich Fromm," in *Contemporary Psychoanalysis*, New York: Academic Press, Vol. 11 (1975), p. 463f.

Freud, S. *The Standard Edition of the Complete Psychological Works of Sigmund Freud* (S. E.), Vol. 1–24, London: Hogarth Press, 1953–1974.

——.1900a: "Dream Interpretation," S. E. Vols. 4 and 5.

——.1919a: "Advances in Psycho-Analytic Therapy," S. E. Vol. 17, pp. 157–168.

——.1937c: "Analysis Terminable and Interminable," S. E. Vol. 23, pp. 209–253.

Fromm, E. 1947a: *Man for Himself: An Inquiry into the Psychology of Ethics*, New York: Rinehart, 1947.

——.1951a: *The Forgotten Language: Introduction to the Understanding of Dreams, Fairy Tales and Myths*, New York: Rinehart, 1951.

——.1956a: *The Art of Loving*, (World Perspectives, Vol. 9, planned and edited by Ruth Nanda Anshen), New York: Harper and Row, 1956.

——.1960a: *Psychoanalysis and Zen Buddhism*, in D. T. Suzuki and E. Fromm *Zen Buddhism and Psychoanalysis*, New York: Harper and Row, 1960, pp. 77–141.

——.1964a: *The Heart of Man: Its Genius for Good and Evil* (Religious Perspectives, Vol. 12, planned and edited by Ruth Nanda Anshen), New York: Harper and Row, 1964.

——.1966f: and Richard I. Evans: *Dialogue with Erich Fromm*, New York: Harper and Row, 1966.

——.1966k: "El complejo de Edipo: Comentarios al 'Analisis de la fobia de un niño de cinco años,'" in *Revista de Psicoanálisis, Psiquiatría y Psicologíia*, México, No. 4 (1966), pp. 26–33; engl.: "The Oedipus Complex: Comments on 'The Case of Little Hans,'" in E. Fromm, *The Crisis of Psychoanalysis* (1970a), pp. 88–99.

——.1970a: *The Crisis of Psychoanalysis, Essays on Freud, Marx and Social Psychology*, New York: Holt, Rinehart and Winston, 1970.

——.1970c: "The Crisis of Psychoanalysis," in E. Fromm, *The Crisis of Psychoanalysis* (1970a), pp. 9–41.

——.1973a: *The Anatomy of Human Destructiveness*, New York: Holt, Rinehart and Winston, 1973.

——.1979a: *Greatness and Limitations of Freud's Thought*, New York: Harper and Row, 1980.

——.1989a: *The Art of Being*, New York: Crossroad / Continuum, 1992.

——.1990a: *The Revision of Psychoanalysis*, Boulder: Westview Press, 1992.

——.1991c: "Causes for the Patient's Change in Analytic Treatment," in *Contemporary Psychoanalysis*, New York: William Alanson White Institute, Vol. 27 (No. 4, October 1991), pp. 581–602.

Funk, R. "Fromm's approach to psychoanalytic theory and its relevance for therapeutic work," in Institutio Mexicano de Psicoanalisis, ed., *El caracter social, su estudio, un intercambio de experiencias*, Coyoacán 1972, pp. 17–43.

Gourevitch, A. "Tribute on Erich Fromm,"in *Contemporary Psychoanalysis*, New York: Academic Press, 1981, Vol. 17, pp. 435–436.

Grey, A. (1992) "Society as Destiny: Erich Fromm's Concept of Social Character,"in *Contemporary Psychoanalysis*, New York: Academic Press, 1992, Vol. 28, pp. 344–363.

——.1993: "The Dialectics of Psychoanalysis: A New Synthesis of Fromm's Theory and Practice," in *Contemporary Psychoanalysis*, New York: William Alanson White Psychoanalytic Society, 1993, Vol. 29, pp. 645–672.

Horney, K. *Self-Analysis*, New York: W. W. Norton, 1942.

Horney Eckardt, M. (1975) L'Chayim. Review of Bernhard Landis and Edward S. Tauber, eds., "In the Name of Life. Essays in Honor of Erich Fromm,"in *Contemporary Psychoanalysis*, New York: Academic Press, 1975, Vol. 11, pp. 465–470.

——.1982: "The Theme of Hope in Erich Fromm's Writing," in *Contemporary Psychoanalysis*, New York: Academic Press, 1982, Vol. 18, pp. 141–152.

——.1983: "The Core Theme of Erich Fromm's Writings and Its Implications for Therapy," in *Journal of the American Academy of Psychoanalysis*, New York: John Wiley & Sons, 1983, Vol. 11, pp. 391–399.

——.1992: "Fromm's Concept of Biophilia," in *Journal of the American Academy of Psychoanalysis*, 1992, Vol. 20, pp. 233–240.

Jung, C. G. *Memories, Dreams, Reflections*, ed. by Aniela Jaffé, New York: Pantheon Books, 1963.

Kretschmer, E. *Körperbau und Charakter*, Berlin: Springer Verlag, 1921.

Kwawer, J. S., (1975) "A Case Seminar with Erich Fromm," in *Contemporary Psychoanalysis*, New York: Academic Press, Vol. 11 (1975), pp. 453–455.

——.(1991) "Fromm on Clinical Psychoanalysis," in *Contemporary Psychoanalysis*, New York: William Alanson White Institute, 1991, Vol. 27, pp. 608–623.

Landis, B. (1975) "Fromm's Theory of Biophilia—Necrophilia. Its Implications for Psychoanalytic Practice," in *Contemporary Psychoanalysis*, New York: Academic Press, 1975, Vol. 11, pp. 418–434.

———.(1981) "Fromm's Approach to Psychoanalytic Technique,"in *Contemporary Psychoanalysis*, New York: Academic Press, 1981, Vol. 17, pp. 537–551.

———.(1981a) "Erich Fromm," in *The William Alanson White Institute Newsletter*, New York, No. 1, Winter 1981, Vol. 15, pp. 2–4.

Lesser, R. M. "Frommian Therapeutic Practice," in *Contemporary Psychoanalysis*, New York: William Alanson White Psychoanalytic Society, 1992, Vol. 28, pp. 483–494.

Luban-Plozza, B., and Egle, U. "Einige Hinweise auf die psychotherapeutische Einstellung und den Interventionsstil von Erich Fromm," in *Patientenbezogene Medizin*, Stuttgart/New York, 1982, Vol. 5, pp. 81–94.

Marx, K. "Zur Kritik der Hegelschen Rechtsphilosophie. Einleitung," in K. Marx and F. Engels, *Historisch-kritische Gesamtausgabe* (= MEGA). Werke—Schriften—Briefe, im Auftrag des Marx-Engels-Lenin-Instituts Moskau, published by V. Adoratskij, 1. Abteilung: SÑmtliche Werke und Schriften mit Ausnahme des Kapital, zit. I, 1–6, Berlin 1932; MEGA I, 1, 1, pp. 607–621.

Nietzsche, F. "Sprüche und Pfeile,"in F. Nietzsche, *Götzendämmerung*.

Norell, M. (1975) "Reminiscences of Supervision with Erich Fromm," in *Contemporary Psychoanalysis*, New York: Academic Press, 1975, Vol. 11, p. 456f.

———.(1981) "Wholly Awake and Fully Alive," in *Contemporary Psychoanalysis*, New York: Academic Press, 1981, Vol. 17, pp. 451–456.

Nyanaponika Mahathera, *The Heart of Buddhist Meditation*, New York: Samuel Weiser, 1973.

Reich, W. *Charakteranalyse: Technik und Grundlagen*, Wien: Verlag für Sexualpolitik, 1933.

Schecter, D. E. (1971) "Of Human Bonds and Bondage," in B. Landis and E.S. Tauber, eds., *In the Name of Life: Essays in Honor of Erich Fromm*, New York: Holt, Rinehart and Winston, 1971, pp. 84–99.

———.(1981) "Tribute on Erich Fromm," in *Contemporary Psychoanalysis*, New York: Academic Press, 1981, Vol. 17, pp. 445–447.

———.(1981a) "Contributions of Erich Fromm," in *Contemporary Psychoanalysis*, New York: Academic Press, 1981, Vol. 17, pp. 468–480.

——.(1981b) "On Fromm," in *The William Alanson White Institute Newsletter*, Vol. 15 (No. 1, Winter 1981), p. 10.

Sheldon, W. H. *The Varieties of Temperament*, New York/London: Harper and Brothers, 1942.

Silva Garcia, J. (1984) "Notes on Psychoanalysis and the Selection of Candidates for Training." Paper presented to the IV. Conferencia Cientifica de la Federación Internacionales de Sociedades Psicoanalísticas, Madrid 1984, p. 18.

——.(1990) "Dreams and Transference," in *American Journal of Psychoanalysis*, New York (1990), Vol. 50, pp. 203–213.

Skinner, B. F. *Beyond Freedom and Dignity*, New York: Knopf, 1971.

Spengler, O. *Untergang des Abendslandes*, 2 Vols., Munich 1918 and 1922.

Spiegel, R. (1981) "Tribute on Erich Fromm," in *Contemporary Psychoanalysis*, New York: Academic Press, 1981, Vol. 17, pp. 436–441.

——.(1983) *Erich Fromm. Humanistic Psychoanalyst 1900–1980. Presentation to the 40th anniversary of the William Alanson White Institute*, New York 1983, p. 5.

Tauber, E. S. (1959) "The Role of Immediate Experience for Dynamic Psychiatry. The Sense of Immediacy in Fromm's Conceptions," in *Handbook of Psychiatry*, New York 1959, pp. 1811–1815.

——.(1979) "Erich Fromm: Clinical and Social Philosopher," in *Contemporary Psychoanalysis*, New York: Academic Press, 1979, Vol. 15, pp. 201–213.

——.(1980) *Fromm—The Man: Presentation in Honor of Erich Fromm at the William Alanson White Institute*, New York, June 18, 1980, p. 3.

——.(1981) "Symbiosis, Narcissism, Necrophilia—Disordered Affect in the Obsessional Character," in *Journal of the American Academy of Psychoanalysis*, New York (1981), Vol. 9, pp. 33–49.

——.(1981a) "Tribute on Erich Fromm," in *Contemporary Psychoanalysis*, New York: Academic Press, 1981, Vol. 17, pp. 448–449.

——.*Psychoanalysis*, New York: William Alanson White Psychoanalytic Society, 1982, Vol. 18, pp. 119–132.

——.(1988) "Exploring the Therapeutic Use of Counter-transference Data," in *Essential Papers On Counter-transference*, ed. by B. Wolstein, New York: New York University Press, 1988, pp. 111–119.

Tauber, E. S., and Landis, B. "On Erich Fromm," in B. Landis and E. S. Tauber, eds., *In the Name of Life: Essays in Honor of Erich Fromm*, New York: Holt, Rinehart and Winston, 1971, pp. 1–11.

Werder, L. von, *Alltägliche Selbstanalyse: Freud—Fromm—Thomas*, ed. L. von Werder, Weinheim: Deutscher Studien Verlag, 1990, p. 239.

Whitehead, A. N. *The Function of Reason*, Boston: Beacon Press, 1967.

Witenberg, E. G. "Tribute on Erich Fromm," in *Contemporary Psychoanalysis*, New York: Academic Press, 1981, Vol. 17, pp. 449–450.

Wolstein, B. "A Historical Note on Erich Fromm: 1955," in *Contemporary Psychoanalysis*, New York: Academic Press, 1981, Vol. 17, pp. 481–485.

Index